THE
ITALIAN
TABLE

THE ITALIAN TABLE

Creating festive meals for family and friends

WRITTEN AND PHOTOGRAPHED BY

Elizabeth Minchilli

New York · Paris · London · Milan

This book is for Domenico,
my favorite dining partner and love of my life.

First published in the United States of America
in 2019
by Rizzoli International Publications, Inc.
300 Park Avenue South
New York, NY 10010
www.rizzoliusa.com

Text and photographs © 2019 Elizabeth Minchilli

2019 2020 2021 2022 / 10 9 8 7 6 5 4 3 2

Distributed in the U.S. trade by Random House,
New York

Printed in China

Design: Toni Tajima

ISBN-13: 978-0-8478-6376-1

Library of Congress Catalog Control Number:
2018960489

CONTENTS

INTRODUCTION

When people visit Italy there are certain cultural monuments that are so huge you can't miss them. The Colosseum, St. Peter's, and the Leaning Tower of Pisa are on everyone's list. And while people come to Italy to eat as well, enjoying pizza, pasta, and gelato at as many meals as possible, they sometimes lose track of how important food is in everyday Italian culture. While the food you put on your plate is very important in Italy, the things that surround that plate—family, friends, and the community and history that make up the meal—is just as crucial. Whether it is a sun-dappled lunch on the beach, a moonlit dinner on a Roman terrace, or a plate of porchetta on a picnic table, Italians bring not just an appetite to any meal, but a sense of occasion, style, and complete and utter joy.

The Italian Table looks at some of these best-loved events, which happen daily in Italy, and translates them into a way of entertaining that you can bring home. By turning these meals into an occasion to invite friends and family around your own table, it is also a chance to capture some of the spirit of the Italian way of life.

It's no secret that Italian food is one of the most popular cuisines in the world, so if you serve your guests pizza, pasta, and gelato, they'll probably be pretty happy. But I think that having a gathering is an opportunity to go beyond the obvious. It's a chance to explore different regional cuisines, from Sicily to the Veneto, and to answer a question about life in Italy that many people remain hungry for: How do Italians actually eat? I receive a version of this question on a daily basis. Do Italians really eat three courses at every meal? Do Italians eat pasta every day? How do Italians stay so thin when it seems to be one big carb fest? Does everyone drink wine with every meal?

Of course there are as many answers as there are questions, but my standard response is as beautifully complex as the country itself. Eating in Italy is as much about the *experience* as it is about the food. Yes, recipes and ingredients are important, but it is the ceremony of the meal itself—or lack of ceremony in most cases—that so often gets left out of the equation once the recipes travel off the peninsula and onto the pages of cookbooks.

This book will explore some of the ways that Italians gather around the table and—importantly—how you can re-create the essence of these experiences at home.

Each meal begins with a brief exploration of what makes up a particular event or dish, but not just from a culinary point of view. For most Italians, the sum of what ends up on the table, and the surrounding joy, has as much to do with an inherited set of cultural touchstones as it does the ingredients. Where do these traditions come from? And what are the elements that come into play when chairs are pulled up to the table? Yes, we'll get to the pasta in that bowl, but what about the bowl itself? And the tool used to get that pasta from bowl to plate? The linens that cover the table—even the simple paper placemats—are intensely local and have a history as well. How do you choose between a chunky glass tumbler or a stemmed wine glass for your red? These are the types of questions that are rarely asked, much less answered, in traditional cookbooks. And knowing the answers to them will enable you to re-create your own Italian gathering at home.

For each event described in this book there are recipes. But just as importantly, there are also game plans that will help you translate these Italian events into a gathering in your own home. Each chapter is divided into sections that cover all the details.

The "Menu" lists each dish in both English and Italian. "Recipe for a Party" explains how to turn this menu into a meal for friends. "Timing" is a key element in making sure you are not stuck in the kitchen, with too much to do, once your guests arrive. And finally, "Inspiration—Set Your Table" will give advice about how to re-create the atmosphere in your own home, with suggestions on everything from centerpieces to table linens. And don't forget "What to Drink": even if it's just sparkling water with a slice of lemon, each Italian meal has its own traditional beverage. (It's usually wine!)

This book is not an encyclopedia of Italian eating. It is a greatest-hits list of some of my favorite meals. Some were in private homes, and some were in restaurants. Some were in the city and some in the country. But one thing they all have in common is that they illustrate how Italians gather around the table. And even if you are not actually at a canal-side bar in Venice, a beachside club in Positano, or a marble table on a Roman rooftop, recipes like pumpkin crostini, mozzarella-topped lemon leaves, and grilled peaches and burrata will make you feel as if you are.

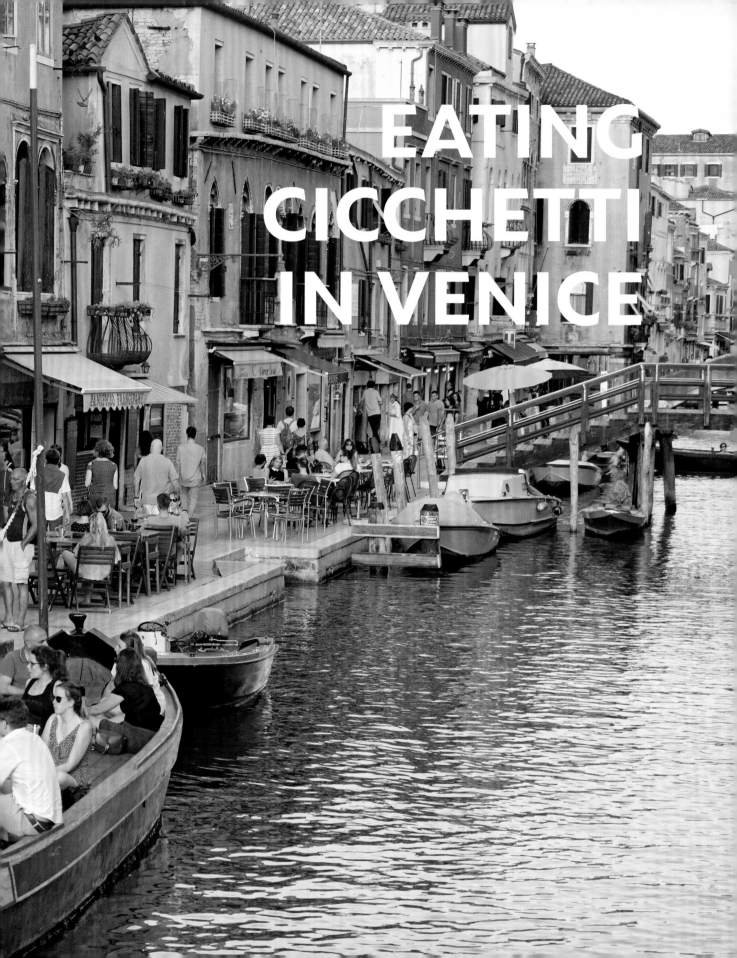

EATING CICCHETTI IN VENICE

Italian isn't a particularly difficult language to learn. You pronounce words the way you read them, and it's a whole lot easier to get the gist of the grammar than in English. But some words, the ones that apply to very specific Italian cultural moments, are challenging to translate. *Passeggiata*, for instance, means a walk. But as all Italians know, *fare la passeggiata* means so much more than taking a walk. It's a chance to see and be seen. You might be taking a walk to head out for a gelato, or maybe to walk off that plate of pasta after a long Sunday lunch. It is always a social occasion.

Food-related words are even more difficult to translate, since they are so intensely regional. For instance, *puntarelle* in Rome refers to a chicory salad that is only available during the winter months. In Umbria? Order a plate of puntarelle and you end up with a big portion of grilled pork ribs.

One word that puzzled me for the longest time was *cicchetti*. Even the spelling (sometimes *cicheti* instead) was confusing. Cicchetti is a word that, until very recently, described a very Venetian thing. The closest I could ever come to a definition was that it was a unique form of tapas—little bites— served in the bars of Venice.

I remember the first time I took what I thought would be a predinner cicchetti stroll in Venice. I headed out at 7:30 only to find that cicchetti hour was drawing to a close. At least that is what I assumed, since some of the places were already shutting down for the day. But as it turns out, even that was misleading. I thought they had started serving cicchetti at "cocktail hour," but that time schedule was open for discussion as well.

I did a bit more digging (that is, eating) and discovered that:

> Cicchetti show up in bars called *bacari* that specialize in them, as well as in some restaurants at certain times of the day, usually late morning or late afternoon into very early evening.

> Cicchetti are chosen from a buffet of plates laid out on the counter.

> Cicchetti are always accompanied by something alcoholic, either an *ombra* (small glass of local wine) or a spritz.

The most important thing I learned, though, was that cicchetti are never meant to be eaten alone. The very nature of eating cicchetti—in a bar surrounded by people—precludes solo dining even if you are on your own: you will end up chatting with strangers whether you like it or not. The entire cicchetti ritual reflects the Italian approach to food and drinking. It's all about getting together with friends for a glass of wine. And since you don't want to drink on an empty stomach, the cicchetti are little nibbles for that exact purpose.

Since my first early and misguided days in Venice, I have logged many hours at the counters of the city's best known bacari. Whether it's a midmorning bite (and a glass of wine) near the Rialto Market to help me make it to lunch, or a cutting-edge array of inventive crostini up in the far reaches of Cannareggio, I have come to embrace the cicchetti lifestyle. I've also managed to bring it back home to Rome with me.

As you can imagine, cicchetti naturally lend themselves to a made-to-order party.

Plates are easily shared, and the variety of ingredients can change to fit any location or season.

In theory almost any small bite can go by the name of cicchetti. I personally like the old-fashioned ones that you find at some of the oldest bacari in Venice, around the Rialto Market. Mostly crostini or *bocconcini* (little bites), they are classics for a reason: they are delicious, easy to eat, and provide ballast for the wine.

Recipe for a Party

Each of the recipes (except the meatballs) makes about eight cicchetti. As a general rule of thumb, you can figure on about eight cicchetti or so per person to make a filling meal (cicchetti are small). This menu, which has nine different recipes, will easily serve eight with some probably left over. The trick to this sit-down party is staggering the plates so that they come out a few at a time. This not only keeps the party going longer (allowing more alcohol to flow), but it also leads to a sense of anticipation as each new set of tidbits lands on the table.

menu

Bocconcini—Little Bites

Mortadella e Peperoni
MORTADELLA AND PICKLED PEPPER 15

Cipolline con Acciughe
PICKLED ONIONS WITH ANCHOVY 16

Uova con Acciughe
EGG WITH ANCHOVY 16

Involtini di Melanzane
EGGPLANT ROLLS 19

Polpettine Fritte
FRIED MEATBALLS 20

Crostini

Crostino di Limone e Cipolle
LEMON AND ONION CROSTINO 23

Crostino di Prosciutto, Ricotta e Melone
PROSCIUTTO, RICOTTA, AND MELON CROSTINO 24

Crostino di Zucca, Ricotta e Parmigiano
PUMPKIN, RICOTTA, AND PARMIGIANO CROSTINO 25

Crostino di Zucchini con Gamberi
MARINATED ZUCCHINI AND RAW SHRIMP CROSTINO 26

what to drink

I would suggest starting out with spritzes for the first "course," then moving on to wine.

Spritzes: Spritzes incorporate a splash of a bitter aperitivo and are now popular throughout Italy. The recipe for a spritz is easy (page 14), but the secret is figuring out which type you like. These days most people choose between Aperol and Campari, but an often-used local ingredient is Select, still made on the Giudecca Island. I am also partial to using Cynar, an artichoke-based amaro.

Wine: If you are a Venetian stopping by your local bacaro on your way home from work, then your drink of choice will be an ombra. *Ombra* translates as "shade," but in Venice it refers to whatever wine is on tap. Today most bacari offer a wide selection of red and white wines, both still and sparking. Venetian wines to try out include Soave, prosecco, and refosco.

timing

This menu is all about the prep. Once you've got your ingredients and have chopped or sliced them, the meal comes together rather easily.

2 DAYS BEFORE

Do your shopping.

1 DAY BEFORE

Hard-boil the eggs. Mix and form the meatballs. Bake and puree the pumpkin and store in an airtight container in the refrigerator. Fry the eggplant. Drain on paper towels and store in an airtight container in the refrigerator.

2 HOURS BEFORE

Bring all of the ingredients to room temperature. Set the table. Marinate the zucchini.

1 HOUR BEFORE

Assemble the Mortadella and Pickled Pepper; Pickled Onions with Anchovy; Egg with Anchovy; and Eggplant Rolls. Fry the meatballs.

WHEN YOUR GUESTS ARRIVE

Once your guests are seated, serve the small dishes in the following order:

First course: Mortadella and Pickled Pepper; Pickled Onions with Anchovy; Egg with Anchovy.

Second course: Eggplant Rolls; Fried Meatballs.

Between the second and third courses, assemble and then serve: Lemon and Onion Crostino; Prosciutto, Ricotta, and Melon Crostino; Pumpkin, Ricotta, and Parmigiano Crostino; and Marinted Zucchini and Raw Shrimp Crostino.

inspiration

SET YOUR TABLE

Keep it simple. The best bacari feel like neighborhood bars (which they are) where plates and utensils are purely optional.

DRESSING YOUR TABLE

Although most bacari use the standard flimsy tissue-like paper napkins found throughout Italy, break out heavier paper napkins. Don't go overboard and use cloth, since this is finger food, and fingers tend to get dirty.

TABLEWARE AND UTENSILS

Simple, heavy white plates will do just fine. The serving platters should be small (holding no more than one recipe's worth). Individual plates should be small since they serve only as a small landing pad for the cicchetti on the way to the mouth. Flatware? No need. This is finger food.

GLASSWARE

Most bacari use stubby little stemmed wine glasses with a small rounded bowl for both red and white wine. And most *ombre* (small glasses of local wine) are filled to the rim, allowing no space for aromas since . . . well, it's not usually that kind of wine. Spritzes are served in large balloon glasses, which leave room for both ice and olives, and this is key, look gorgeous.

Spritz

Spritzes are just fun to drink. A mixture of fizzy wine and brightly colored amaro served in an ice-filled goblet, this drink feels unquestionably festive. While most Italians will garnish theirs with a slice of orange, in Venice spritzes always come adorned with a few big green olives, which make perfect sense to balance out the slightly sweet, yet bitter, flavor of the drink. SERVES 1

3 parts prosecco or other dry sparkling white wine

2 parts Aperol or Campari

Splash of soda water

Big green olives with the pit, such as Castelvetrano from Sicily

Fill a large wine goblet with ice. Pour in the prosecco and then the Aperol. Top up with soda water to halfway to three-quarters of the way up the glass. The exact quantities depend on how big your glass is, and how strong you would like your drink. Garnish with some big green olives on a toothpick.

Bocconcini
LITTLE BITES

Bocconcini translates as "small bites" and refers to a class of cicchetti that are served without bread, and which usually consist of something sweet or sour with something salty and/or fatty. These simple concoctions hit just the right spot with a spritz, Negroni, or a simple glass of prosecco.

While many cicchetti are served with toothpicks to transfer the food from the plate to your mouth, here toothpicks are also an essential element for keeping the ingredients together.

Bocconcini are barely-there recipes, usually simply two or three ingredients. Here are my favorites, which happen to be classics. **EACH RECIPE MAKES 8 CICCHETTI**

Mortadella e Peperoni
MORTADELLA AND PICKLED PEPPER

The pairing of salty and fatty with crispy and sour is a good one, and it gets repeated often with bocconcini in Venice. The trick is getting the right quantities of each element so they balance each other out. When you buy your mortadella at the deli, ask the person helping you to cut it 1 inch thick. You do not want paper-thin slices of mortadella for this dish. Since mortadella is usually very large in diameter you will probably have some left over after you make the cicchetti. And so, you will have to eat it—which is not too much of a sacrifice.

One 1-inch-thick slice of mortadella

One 8- or 12-ounce jar of Italian pickled green peppers, drained

Cut the mortadella into small wedges; they should be about ½ inch wide at the widest end and as long as your peppers (about 1½ inches).

Place 1 pepper atop each piece of mortadella and secure with a toothpick.

Cipolline con Acciughe

PICKLED ONIONS WITH ANCHOVY

This is one of my favorite bites in Venice. My love for it has something to do with the mix of slightly sweet-and-sour onion with briny anchovy. I almost always use jarred onions, which are available in Italian specialty shops, and are usually packed in olive oil. Do not confuse these with the small martini onions that are packed in brine.

(pictured page 18, right)

8 to 16 preserved Italian cipolline onions

8 anchovy fillets

8 Italian pickled green peppers (optional)

Depending on how big your onions are or how you want this to look, you can top each onion with an anchovy and call it quits, sandwich the anchovy between two onions, or top the onion and anchovy with a green pepper. In each case, roll up the anchovy before securing it to the onion(s) with the toothpick.

Uova con Acciughe

EGG WITH ANCHOVY

Here's another one you'll see at every cicchetti place you visit—and with good reason. Remember, the point of stopping by a bacaro is to have a glass of wine. Eggs are a great absorber of alcohol—think about those jars of pickled eggs in pubs. As with all things simple, though, the trick is in the quality of the ingredients. Use farm-fresh eggs topped with imported, high-quality anchovies.

(pictured opposite)

4 large eggs, at room temperature

8 anchovy fillets

Place the eggs in a medium pot and cover with enough cold water to come up 1 inch over the top of the eggs. Turn the heat to medium-high and bring the water to a boil. Cover the pan, remove it immediately from the heat, and set it aside for 10 minutes.

In the meantime, prepare a bowl of ice water.

Drain the eggs and place them in the ice water. Let sit until cold.

Peel the eggs and cut them carefully in half lengthwise. Place them on a plate. There are two ways to lay the anchovy atop the egg: either keep the anchovy flat, letting it flop over the sides of the egg, or roll the anchovy up first. Then secure it with a toothpick by sticking the toothpick into the yolk of the egg.

Involtini di Melanzane

EGGPLANT ROLLS

During the summer months, eggplants show up as part of the cicchetti offerings all over Venice. Sometimes they are mini eggplant parmigiano, other times they get chopped up and fried into a little bite-sized ball. These simple *involtini* (rolls) are served often at one of the oldest bacari in Venice, Cantina Do Mori, and are one of my favorites. They don't actually add basil to theirs, but I think it seems almost criminal not to. **MAKES 8 ROLLS**

(pictured opposite, left)

1 medium eggplant, sliced into ¼- to ½-inch rounds (you will need 8 rounds)

Sea salt

3 ounces of fresh mozzarella

1½ to 2 cups of extra-virgin olive oil

8 fresh basil leaves

8 oil-packed sun-dried tomatoes, drained

Lightly salt the eggplant rounds (use about 1½ teaspoons) and let them drain in a colander over a bowl for 45 minutes. After they have sweated out their liquid, blot them dry with paper towels.

In the meantime, cut the mozzarella into ½-inch slices and then into ½-inch strips. Place in a sieve over a bowl to drain for 15 to 20 minutes.

Pour the olive oil into a large frying pan to a depth of 1½ to 2 inches. Line a plate with paper towels. Heat the oil to 320° to 340°F or until it begins to shimmer and a fleck of water immediately sizzles. Fry the eggplant rounds in batches. Do not overcrowd the pan. After about 5 minutes, flip the rounds over and continue cooking until tender, another 3 to 4 minutes. Remove from the oil using a slotted spoon and place on the paper towels to drain. Lightly season with salt. Repeat until you've fried all of the rounds. Let cool completely. If making a day ahead, cover and store in the refrigerator.

To assemble the involtini, once the eggplant has cooled, place 1 or 2 strips of mozzarella in the center of an eggplant round and roll it up. Place 1 basil leaf and 1 sun-dried tomato on top and secure it all with a toothpick. Repeat for the remaining rounds. Serve immediately.

Polpettine Fritte

FRIED MEATBALLS

Meatballs in Italy come in all shapes and sizes. With sauce and without, fried, baked, and sometimes even finding their way into pasta. But perhaps my all-time favorite meatballs are the tiny deep-fried ones served as cicchetti at the restaurant Cà D'Oro alla Vedova in Venice. They are crispy-crunchy on the outside, tender and perfectly seasoned on the inside. The exact recipe is super secret, but this one comes pretty close, I think. MAKES 30 TO 40 MINI MEATBALLS

1 small potato

½ cup of whole milk

½ slice of day-old rustic bread

1 pound of ground beef

2 cloves of garlic, finely chopped

3 large eggs

1 teaspoon of sea salt

¼ teaspoon of freshly ground black pepper

1 ounce of Parmigiano-Reggiano, grated (¼ cup)

¼ cup of chopped fresh Italian flat-leaf parsley

4 cups of organic sunflower seed oil or other neutral-tasting oil, for frying

1 cup of all-purpose flour

1½ cups of dried breadcrumbs

Bring a pot of water to a boil. Leaving the skin on, boil the potato until tender, about 20 minutes. Remove from the heat and let sit until the potato is cool enough to handle. Slip the skin off, discard it, and place the potato in a large bowl. Use a fork to mash thoroughly, removing any lumps.

In the meantime, pour the milk into a small bowl and soak the bread in it for 15 minutes.

Add the beef, garlic, 1 of the eggs, the salt, pepper, Parmigiano, and parsley to the potato. Squeeze any excess milk out of the bread, discard the milk, and add the bread. Using your hands, mix the ingredients until they form a smooth paste.

Form a meatball by rolling 1 to 2 tablespoons of the mixture between your hands. It should be about 1 inch in diameter. Place it on a plate. Repeat until you have used all the meat mixture. Cover the plate of meatballs with plastic wrap and put them in the refrigerator to chill for at least 2 hours.

When you are ready to fry, pour the oil into a medium pot and heat it to about 330°F, or until a drop of water sizzles.

Put the flour, the 2 remaining eggs, and the breadcrumbs in three separate small bowls. Beat the eggs well with a fork to break them up.

Line a plate with paper towels. When the oil is hot, remove the meatballs from the refrigerator. Dip a few first in the flour, then in the egg, and finally in the breadcrumbs, coating them well each time. Gently slip them into the hot oil and fry until golden brown, about 5 minutes. Remove from the oil with a slotted spoon and place on the paper towels to drain. Don't fry too many at once. You will probably have to fry them in three or four batches.

Transfer the meatballs to a serving plate, stick toothpicks in them, and serve immediately. They are best when eaten hot or at room temperature.

Crostini

The crostino is the Venetian cicchetti that you will find in every single *bacaro* throughout Venice. At its most basic it is a piece of bread with something on it. But within that narrow definition there are, of course, infinite variations that can result in anything from a piece of stale or soggy bread topped with dried ham to a perfectly toasted slice of sourdough whole wheat baguette crowned by marinated, freshly caught sardines.

After intense "research" into what makes one crostino better than the rest, here are a few rules I've picked up.

Bread: Most of the crostini you'll see are served atop slices of baguette. These days most baguettes (not a typical or local loaf) are semi-industrially produced. The really great ones are artisanally made and so have a crisp crust and a compact crumb that is slightly sour, and they don't turn to mush and/or go stale the minute they are sliced and then topped.

Another alternative that I often saw was the use of oblong or round rolls. These were cut in half horizontally, and then each half was cut into three or four pieces (not slices) so that each crostino base had the crusty exterior part of the roll on the outside, while the topping was sitting on the crumb.

Timing: Across the board, the best crostini are made within 15 minutes or less of being consumed. No crostino can stand the test of time, no matter how delicious the topping. The best ones I've ever had were made to order just for me.

Bellezza **(Beauty):** It goes without saying that the ingredients have to be top-notch, but once you're at that stage the construction of the crostino should be a little work of art. Think about tastes and textures, of course, but color and shape also play an important role.

Giving a "recipe" for a crostino seems almost silly, but here are a few I had in Venice that followed all the rules and will give you a great starting point.

Crostino di Limone e Cipolle

LEMON AND ONION CROSTINO

I had these clever little crostini while sailing across the Venetian lagoon on an antique fishing boat. Mauro Stoppa is both the captain and the chef of the charming boat, the *Eolo*, which takes visitors out to explore the far reaches of the lagoon. As we headed off, he popped open a bottle of prosecco and handed around a plate of these crostini to nibble on. Rather than use slices of fresh bread, he uses mini friselle, a type of twice-baked bread, which are really little crisp crackers. If you can't find friselle, then you can substitute any sort of rustic, thick cracker. Or if you feel inspired to bake your own, see page 222.

MAKES 12 CROSTINI

- **1 teaspoon of sea salt**
- **1 medium white onion**
- **1 large organic, unsprayed lemon (if using a conventional lemon, scrub it well and dry it)**
- **½ cup of loosely packed fresh mint leaves, plus 12 more for garnish**
- **2 tablespoons of extra-virgin olive oil**
- **12 mini friselle, rusks, or other type of rustic cracker**

Dissolve ½ teaspoon of the salt in a small bowl of water. Thinly slice the onion into half-rounds. Soak the onions in the salted water for 30 minutes. Drain, rinse them off, and pat them dry with paper towels.

Slice the lemon into paper-thin rounds. Make sure you remove all of the seeds. Cut each round in half, and those halves into thirds, so you have little wedges.

Place the lemon wedges in a small bowl. Gently tear the mint leaves by hand into smaller pieces and add them to the lemon. Add the onion, olive oil, and the remaining ½ teaspoon of salt and mix gently. Cover the bowl and marinate at room temperature for 1 hour.

About 15 minutes before you are ready to serve the crostini, place the rusks on a small serving platter or plate. Top each rusk with a spoonful of the mixture. Let them sit for 15 minutes to soften the cracker a bit. Top each with a fresh whole mint leaf and serve.

Crostino di Prosciutto, Ricotta e Melone

PROSCIUTTO, RICOTTA, AND MELON CROSTINO

The appetizer of prosciutto and melon can be found all over Italy, all summer long, when melons are ripe and juicy. The pairing is one of the few salty and sweet combinations that most Italians love. This classic easily turns into a cicchetti with the addition of a little fresh ricotta to keep everything in place. I personally love the touch of using balls of melon, even if they do tend to roll off!

MAKES 8 CROSTINI

1 cup of fresh ricotta

¼ of a melon, such as cantaloupe or honeydew

8 slices of Prosciutto di Parma

½ of a good-quality baguette

8 fresh marjoram or mint leaves, for garnish

Put the ricotta in a fine sieve over a bowl and let drain for 2 hours.

Place the drained ricotta into a small bowl, and whip it with a fork until smooth.

Using a melon baller, scoop out 8 small balls of melon.

Cut the baguette on the diagonal into eight ½-inch-thick slices.

Lay 1 slice of prosciutto on top of each slice of bread, folding it over to fit. Using a soup spoon, place some ricotta in the middle of the prosciutto. Place the melon ball on top of the ricotta, pushing it down a bit so it doesn't roll off. Place a marjoram leaf on top of the melon. Serve immediately.

Crostino di Zucca, Ricotta e Parmigiano

PUMPKIN, RICOTTA, AND PARMIGIANO CROSTINO

Zucca, or pumpkin, is much more common in Northern Italy than in the south. One of the most common ways to find it is mixed with ricotta and tucked inside ravioli. This recipe takes those flavors and turns them into a crostino.

MAKES 8 CROSTINI

- **1 cup of fresh ricotta**
- **½ of a good-quality baguette**
- **1 cup of winter squash puree (preferably butternut; see Note)**
- **4 ounces of Parmigiano-Reggiano, grated (1 cup)**
- **Freshly ground black pepper**

Place the ricotta in a fine sieve over a bowl and let drain for 2 hours.

Transfer the drained ricotta to a small bowl and whip it with a fork until smooth.

Cut the baguette on the diagonal into eight ½-inch slices. Spread each with about a tablespoon of ricotta, and then place a dollop of the squash puree in the middle. Shower liberally with grated Parmigiano and a few pinches of black pepper.

NOTE To make your own butternut squash puree, preheat the oven to 350°F. Cover a baking sheet with parchment paper. Cut a butternut squash in half lengthwise, and scoop out the seeds. Coat it with olive oil and place it cut side down on the baking sheet. Bake until tender, 45 minutes to an hour. Remove from the oven and let cool. Scoop out the flesh and put it in a food processor, with 2 teaspoons of olive oil and ¼ teaspoon of salt. Process until completely smooth.

Crostino di Zucchini con Gamberi

MARINATED ZUCCHINI AND RAW SHRIMP CROSTINO

This delicacy is the creative invention of the bacaro Cantina, which prides itself on made-to-order cicchetti. Each one is a little work of art, and all of the ingredients are paired in inventive ways that you rarely see atop a cicchetti. This one, which marries raw shrimp with barely marinated zucchini, is one of my favorites. Use high-quality shrimp.

MAKES 8 CROSTINI

1 medium zucchini

Juice of 1 lemon

2 teaspoons of sea salt

2 or 3 shishito peppers, stemmed and seeded

½ of a whole wheat baguette

8 fresh shrimp or prawns, cleaned, peeled, and deveined

Extra-virgin olive oil, for drizzling

Fleur de sel or other flaky finishing salt

Slice the zucchini into ⅛-inch rounds and put them in a small bowl. Pour the lemon juice over, add the sea salt, and toss very gently. Let them marinate for at least a half hour but no more than 2 hours at room temperature.

Using a very sharp knife, slice the peppers into very thin ribbons and set aside.

Cut the baguette on the diagonal into eight ½-inch slices. Gently toast the baguette slices.

Drain the zucchini and discard the marinade. Blot the zucchini dry with paper towels. Place a few slices of zucchini on each slice of bread, then top each with 1 shrimp. Drizzle lightly with olive oil and season to taste with sea salt. Garnish each with a few strips of pepper. Serve immediately.

SUNDAY LUNCH IN EMILIA-ROMAGNA

Even though families in Italy gather around the table daily for meals, traditions have changed quite a bit in the last few decades. Before World War II it was normal for the man of the house to head off for work while the women did the daily shopping and then cooked the big meal of the day: lunch. Most workers, from laborers to lawyers, would go back home if they could to sit down to a two- or three-course meal, which would be followed by a much-needed siesta. My mother-in-law, who grew up with this schedule and then repeated it in her own household, still can't seem to wrap her head around the fact that I don't spend my mornings cooking.

These days not only do most women work outside the house, but neither men nor women stop what they are doing at 1:00 pm to close up shop for a long, drawn-out lunch. Instead, a quick sandwich, or even a plate of pasta or piece of pizza, is eaten during a lunch break and then it's back to work, with a bigger meal happening at home for dinner. But even these evening meals tend to be smaller, less complicated affairs, especially on weeknights.

At least once a week, though, the tradition of a long meal continues. Gathering the extended family around the table for a big Sunday lunch is a practice that continues all over Italy, in the city and in the countryside, in the north and in the south. Sundays, at least for now, are mostly a day of rest. And so, naturally, a day of eating.

Nowhere is the tradition of Sunday lunch more alive than in the region of Emilia-Romagna, where many of the country's best-loved ingredients (like Parmigiano-Reggiano, Aceto Balsamico Tradizionale di Modena, and Prosciutto di Parma) come from. The keepers of the flame of family cooking in this part of the world are called *rezdore*. Loosely translated, *rezdora* means "housewife" but with a strong emphasis on one part of the house: the kitchen. While rezdore were in charge of much more than just cooking, the image that comes to mind is a strong, robust woman who spends at least part of her day rolling out sheets of paper-thin pasta for her family's meals.

Nowadays true rezdore are few and far between. Luckily my friend Maria Chiara (who works with the Parmigiano-Reggiano Consortium) knows quite a few. Maria Chiara is from a very small town just south of Parma. She grew up fascinated by the life these women still keep alive on a daily basis. Staying at home, they make sure their families are fed the way families have been eating in this part of the world for generations. The recipes they use come from handwritten books passed down from mother to daughter, and they proudly source the ingredients from the land that surrounds them.

That said, even their lives have changed with the times. The main meal of the day usually happens in the evenings, when husbands and children come home from work and school. But come Sunday, the main dining room is set with a freshly pressed cloth, the good dishes are brought out, and—of course—handmade pasta and a roast of some kind take center stage.

The following menu is the result of two different meals I enjoyed with two different rezdore, Rina and Maria Elisa.

Recipe for a Party

Sunday lunch in Italy easily translates into a meal to serve your guests for a special, somewhat formal, occasion. While I usually try to simplify menus to make entertaining easier, this menu makes no concession to ease. I'm asking you to channel your inner rezdora and pull out all the stops to make your guests feel like much-loved family.

This menu does include homemade pasta; no Sunday lunch in this part of the world would be complete without it. And if you've never made it before, I can understand if you are a bit intimidated. If you want to substitute store-bought ravioli for the homemade tortelli you can . . . but may I try to convince you to take this opportunity to learn something new? Fair warning, though: before you attempt to make these tortelli for a dinner for guests, give it a go at least two times.

menu

{*Pane*—Crusty Italian Bread}

Antipasto

{Prosciutto di Parma}

Radicchio con Pancetta e Parmigiano
RADICCHIO WITH PANCETTA AND PARMIGIANO 34

Primo

Tortelli di Erbette
RICOTTA AND SWISS CHARD—FILLED TORTELLI 37

Secondi

Arrosto di Maiale con Mortadella
STUFFED PORK ROAST WITH MORTADELLA 40

Torta di Spinaci
SPINACH TART 43

Dolce

Torta allo Sassolino
SPONGE CAKE WITH ANISE LIQUEUR 44

what to drink

WINE

Lambrusco is both the name of a grape and the wine that is made from it. The grapes come from the regions surrounding Parma and the slightly fizzy, dry red wine shows up at virtually every meal. The drier, newer versions of Lambrusco are excellent, and the perfect thing to pair with the rich food of this region. And remember, even though this is a red wine, it is meant to be slightly chilled.

DIGESTIVO

If ever there was a land where you need an after-dinner drink to help digest your meal this is it. The meat- and cheese-heavy dishes of this area call for at least one small glass of herb-filled amaro to help settle the stomach. Bargnolino is an extremely local after-dinner drink made at home from wild plums. It's difficult to find outside of the region, though; an equally delicious (and effective) alternative is nocino, a digestif made from unripe walnuts.

timing

1 DAY BEFORE

Bake the Sponge Cake. Set the table (you might as well get this out of the way). Make the Spinach Tart. Prepare and stuff the pork roast, and put it in the refrigerator.

4 HOURS BEFORE

Make the tortelli, up to the point of boiling them. Store them in the refrigerator or in a cool place.

2 HOURS BEFORE

Take the pork roast out of the refrigerator. Prepare the radicchio up until the cooking. Prepare and trim the vegetables for the pork roast.

1 HOUR BEFORE

Preheat the oven and cook the pork roast.

WHEN YOUR GUESTS ARRIVE

Cook the radicchio. While you are eating your antipasto, bring a large pot of water to a boil for the tortelli. Cook the tortelli, melt the butter, and serve. Place the spinach tart in the oven to reheat while eating the tortelli.

inspiration

SET YOUR TABLE

Just as people wear their Sunday best to church, families tend to set their tables with a bit more care on Sundays. The best plates, the silver, and the crystal get dusted off. The tablecloth is not just startling white, but also ironed to crisp perfection.

DRESSING YOUR TABLE

At rezdora Rina's home, which is a modern building on the outskirts of the village, her dining table was laid with a mixture of old and new. A crisp hand-embroidered tablecloth was part of her original dowry (yes, those still exist!) while the plates with flowered borders are a more modern addition. Instead of choosing which plates go with which tablecloth, she made an effort to bring out the nicest objects from her cupboard.

The point here is not to use your everyday china. If you don't have a special set, maybe it's time you did? I am a big believer in tag sales, where entire sets of plates can be picked up for next to nothing. EBay also becomes addictive once you decide on a pattern you like.

Radicchio con Pancetta e Parmigiano Reggiano

RADICCHIO WITH PANCETTA AND PARMIGIANO

This little dish was made by the rezdora Maria Elisa as a start to our lunch at her home in the hills outside of Parma. Like many of the dishes she prepares for her extended family, she invented this recipe based on extremely local ingredients put together in a new way. Of course Parmigiano-Reggiano makes its way into this dish (as it does most dishes in the region) but instead of using prosciutto, for this dish Maria Elisa chooses its fattier cousin: pancetta. Made from the belly of the pig, the fatty cut of cured meat wraps the bitter leaves and keeps in the filling—which is basically more pancetta!

Make sure you use radicchio di Treviso for this dish, the type of radicchio with long, pliant leaves. It is a variety that is particularly sweet and tender, and unlike the tougher and more bitter round heads of Chioggia. If you can't find radicchio di Treviso, you can use Belgian endive (which is actually a variety of chicory, as is radicchio). And while Maria Elisa used local walnuts, I've often made it with hazelnuts. **SERVES 8**

4 heads of radicchio di Treviso, leaves separated

30 thin slices of pancetta (about ½ pound)

Sea salt and freshly ground black pepper

Extra-virgin olive oil

8 shelled walnuts, roughly chopped

4 ounces of Parmigiano-Reggiano, grated (1 cup)

Preheat the oven to 325°F.

Line a baking sheet with parchment paper and lay the radicchio leaves on top. If some of the inner leaves are very small, you can put two together to make a larger base.

Fry half of the pancetta in a nonstick frying pan over medium heat until it has released its fat a bit. Don't let it burn. You won't need any oil, since the pancetta should be pretty fatty. This may need to be done in a few batches. Each batch should only take a few minutes.

Season the radicchio with salt and pepper and drizzle with olive oil. Distribute the cooked pancetta on top of each leaf, then add the chopped nuts and sprinkle with the Parmigiano.

Wrap each stuffed leaf with a slice of uncooked pancetta. Bake for about 20 minutes, until the pancetta around the outside is cooked and beginning to sizzle. Serve immediately, while warm.

Tortelli di Erbette

RICOTTA AND SWISS CHARD–FILLED TORTELLI

Almost every housewife in this part of the world can roll out a sheet of pasta in her sleep. Making pasta dough gets passed down from mother to daughter, and no one thinks twice about whipping up a batch of freshly made pasta for a meal. That said, tortelli, which are stuffed with a mixture of ricotta and some sort of vegetable, are definitely on the special occasion side of things.

What differentiates these stuffed ravioli from ones in Florence or Rome is the larger ratio of Parmigiano-Reggiano in the filling mixture. Since the finished tortelli will taste mostly of the Parmigiano inside, make sure you use the best you can find— ideally, one that is between eighteen and twenty-four months old. At the end of the process, the tortelli should be swimming in butter, which the additional grated cheese it is served with will soak up.

If you are afraid of attempting homemade pasta, I can relate. I too was mystified at first and had a few disasters. But in this case, practice really does make perfect, and once you get the hang of it, it really is easy. If you know someone who is an expert, it's worthwhile hanging out in his or her kitchen to watch and to feel the dough. During the course of my time spent in the kitchens of rezdore outside of Parma, I learned a huge amount. **SERVES 4 OR 5**

NOTE For years I used a hand-cranked machine for my homemade pasta efforts. (The most common brand is Imperia.) I managed to hold the pasta dough with one hand, feeding it into the machine while cranking with the other, and wishing with all my heart that I had a third hand to catch the dough as it came out. I finally broke down and bought a motor to attach to my machine. It changed my life. So if you are going to buy a machine, a motor is your friend.

A pasta-making board is also helpful. These boards are usually thinner than cutting boards (about ½ inch) and usually measure about 2 x 3 feet. One edge should have a wooden lip that hangs over the edge of your counter, which keeps the board from moving while you are kneading and rolling.

{ *continues* }

3 cups of all-purpose flour, plus more for the work surface

4 large eggs

1 pound of Swiss chard or spinach

1¼ cups of fresh ricotta

12 ounces of Parmigiano-Reggiano, grated (3 cups)

1 large egg yolk

Sea salt, for the cooking water

1 cup (2 sticks) of unsalted butter

Lightly flour a pasta-making board.

Pour the flour into a wide bowl and make a well in the center. Add the 4 whole eggs in the center and, with a fork, gradually work in the flour from the sides. Once it is all incorporated, turn the dough onto the floured board and use your hands to knead the dough until it is smooth and elastic. If at the beginning it seems a bit too dry, you can add a couple of drops of water.

Form the dough into a disk, wrap it in plastic, and let rest at room temperature for 30 minutes.

In the meantime, make the filling: Wash the Swiss chard and remove any big, tough stems. Place it in a pot with about an inch of water, and cook over medium heat for 10 minutes, until completely wilted. Drain and, when cool enough to handle, squeeze the water out of it completely.

Place the chard on a cutting board and roughly chop it. Don't chop it too finely, since you'll want to see flecks of green in the finished pasta.

Place the Swiss chard in a bowl, add the ricotta, and mix well with a fork. Add the egg yolk and 1½ cups of the Parmigiano, and mix well.

Prepare a lightly floured surface (the pasta board or a wooden countertop) and a lightly floured baking sheet.

Cut off a bit of the dough, about a fistful. Re-cover the remaining dough with plastic so it doesn't dry out while you work.

On the lightly floured surface, roll out the piece of dough to flatten it into an oblong shape about ¼ inch thick. Set your pasta machine on the thickest setting, and run the pasta through it. Fold the two ends in to meet at the center and run it through two more times, repeating the folding, two more times. This part is actually kneading the dough.

Now change the machine to a thinner setting, running the dough through again with no folding. Repeat, changing to a thinner setting each time. When the dough becomes too long to handle, you can cut it in half to make it easier. Once the dough is on the next-to-thinnest setting, lay out the strip of dough on the floured surface, with the long side facing you.

Scoop up some of the filing with a large soup spoon, then, using a smaller spoon, push walnut-sized drops of filling along the center of the strip of pasta dough, leaving 1 to 1½ inches between the drops.

Pick up the long edge of the pasta that is closest to you, and bring it up and over the filling to the far edge, pressing down at the edge so it sticks. Using the little finger of your right hand as an edge, make a **C** and cup your hand around the edges of the filling, pushing down, to remove any air pockets between the filling and the dough.

Using a fluted pasta cutting wheel, divide the strip into individual tortelli, sealing the edges and cutting them with the wheel at the same time.

Gently transfer the finished tortelli to the floured pan, in a single layer, until ready to cook. Repeat with the rest of the dough and filling. If the tortelli are too crowded, use an additional pan.

Bring a large pot of salted water to a boil.

Gently melt the butter over very low heat (I sometimes just use the microwave).

Carefully drop the tortelli in the boiling water in two or three batches. They will only take 3 to 4 minutes to cook.

Pour a bit of the melted butter into a large serving bowl. Scoop up the cooked tortelli from the boiling water with a slotted spoon and put into the bowl. Finish cooking the rest of the pasta and keep adding more butter as you transfer the cooked tortelli to the serving bowl.

Bring the bowl to the table immediately and serve the tortelli one by one using a fork, so as not to break them. Pass the remaining 1½ cups Parmigiano at the table.

Arrosto di Maiale con Mortadella

STUFFED ROAST PORK WITH MORTADELLA

Some sort of roast is always the centerpiece of a Sunday family meal in almost all regions of Italy. Traditionally, because meat was such a precious ingredient, especially in the poorer southern regions, you'll often see that the meat used to flavor the pasta sauce for the *primo* turns up again as the main course. And any leftovers are used the next day in inventive and parsimonious recipes. Even though things have changed, these traditions persist.

Farther north, in this part of the world, where a richer way of eating reflects both a higher income as well as more plentiful amounts of meat, the main dish often highlights meat in a completely extravagant way. The day I lunched at Rina's house, she didn't simply make a pork roast, but prepared an intricately assembled pork roast that was stuffed not only with more meat, but with eggs and cheese as well.

In a feat of bravura cookery Rina used a slurry of eggs and cheese to stuff the tenderloin, somehow managing not to let any of the runny filling slip out the ends. But I choose the coward's way (which, frankly, is just as delicious) by making a frittata first to assure none of the precious stuffing escapes. SERVES 8

(pictured pages 28–29)

Two 1½-pound pork tenderloins, butterflied (see Note, opposite)

Sea salt and freshly ground black pepper

2 large eggs

4 ounces of Parmigiano-Reggiano, grated (1 cup)

1 tablespoon plus 2 teaspoons of extra-virgin olive oil

8 thin slices of mortadella

4 ounces of fine, dried breadcrumbs (about ⅓ cup)

1 medium bell pepper, any color

1 medium eggplant

2 medium potatoes

2 medium carrots

2 medium white onions

2 stalks of celery

2 medium zucchini

4 tablespoons (½ stick) of unsalted butter

4 cloves of garlic, peeled

8 cherry tomatoes

Take the tenderloins out of the refrigerator about an hour before you are going to prepare them.

Cover the top of the meat with plastic wrap and, using the flat side of a meat mallet, pound the piece of meat to even it out. It should be about ½ inch thick; repeat with the other piece of meat. Season each lightly with salt and pepper and let sit for 45 minutes.

To make the frittatas: Break 1 egg into a small bowl and mix with ¼ cup of the Parmigiano. Heat a small nonstick frying pan (about 8 inches in diameter) with 1 teaspoon olive oil. Add the egg mixture, swirling the pan to coat the bottom. Let cook until set, 3 to 4 minutes. Remove the frittata from the pan and let cool. Repeat with the other egg, another teaspoon of olive oil, and another ¼ cup Parmigiano to make a second frittata.

Sprinkle the remaining Parmigiano over the open pork fillets. Layer half of the mortadella and then one frittata on top of each. Sprinkle each with half of the breadcrumbs.

Carefully roll up one of the tenderloins, starting at a long side, making sure that none of the stuffing comes out of either end. Using kitchen twine, securely tie up the stuffed roast. If you have a cook's needle you can use this to make sure the roast is tightly bound. Repeat for the other tenderloin. If preparing the day before, wrap in plastic and store in the fridge.

Cut the bell pepper, eggplant, potatoes, carrots, onions, celery, and zucchini into 1-inch pieces.

Preheat the oven to 350°F.

Pour the tablespoon of olive oil into an ovenproof casserole, add the butter, and place over medium-high heat. Add the tenderloins, along with 2 of the garlic cloves. Brown the meat well on all sides. Once the meat is well browned, 8 to 10 minutes, remove the garlic cloves, and

add the vegetables to the pan along with the remaining 2 garlic cloves. Stir the vegetables around the meat with a wooden spoon, deglazing the pan. Add a bit of water if the pan seems dry.

Season the vegetables with salt, stir, and then transfer the pan to the oven. Roast for 40 to 50 minutes, until the vegetables are cooked through.

Remove from the oven and let rest for 10 minutes.

Cut off the twine and carefully slice the roast into ½-inch-thick slices. Place on a serving platter, surrounded by the vegetables.

NOTE To butterfly the pork, lay each tenderloin on a flat surface. Make a 1-inch-deep cut down the center, being careful not to cut all the way through. Open up the meat, spreading both parts to the side, like a book.

VARIATION

If you have non-pork eaters in your family, you can substitute a skinless, boneless butterflied turkey breast or leg for the tenderloin, and eliminate the mortadella. If using turkey breast, reduce the cooking time by about 10 minutes, or else it will dry out. If using the leg then the timing remains unchanged.

Torta di Spinaci

SPINACH TART

This recipe is called a tart, but it's really more of a flan, made without a crust. The vegetables are mixed with ricotta and eggs and just a bit of flour before being baked. The result is a sort of rustic soufflé. I enjoyed this dish at rezdora Maria Elisa's home in the countryside. The day I visited, we went into the woods to gather the vegetables: wild nettles. If you can find nettles, then by all means use them (make sure to wear gloves when you wash them to avoid being stung). Otherwise, another leafy green like spinach or Swiss chard will do. Maria Elisa served this as a side dish, but since it's so cheesy I think it would work as part of an antipasto as well. It is also substantial enough to eat on its own for lunch with a big green salad. **SERVES 8**

About 2 pounds of spinach or other greens

1 cup of fresh ricotta

1 large egg

1 large egg yolk

½ cup of whole milk

4 tablespoons of extra-virgin olive oil

4 ounces of Parmigiano-Reggiano, grated (1 cup)

1 tablespoon of fresh marjoram leaves (or ½ teaspoon dried)

4 tablespoons (½ stick) of salted butter, melted

½ teaspoon of sea salt

A few grindings of black pepper

Place the greens in a pot with about an inch of water and cook over medium heat for about 10 minutes, until wilted. Drain, and when cool enough to handle, squeeze the greens into a ball, squeezing out every last drop of moisture.

You should have about 1 cup. Roughly chop the greens and set aside.

About an hour before you are going to bake the tart, place the ricotta in a fine sieve and drain it over a bowl to remove the excess whey.

Preheat the oven to 350°F. Line the bottom of a 9-inch round cake pan with parchment paper.

Put the chopped greens in clean bowl with the drained ricotta, whole egg and yolk, milk, 3 tablespoons of the olive oil, ¾ cup of the Parmigiano, the marjoram, butter, salt, and pepper. Mix well with a fork.

Pour the mixture into the pan, leveling off the top with the back of a spoon. Cover with the remaining olive oil and Parmigiano.

Bake for 50 minutes, until the tart begins to brown and is well set. Remove from the oven and let cool for 10 minutes. Loosen the sides with a knife and, using an offset spatula, turn it out onto a serving platter. Serve.

Torta allo Sassolino
SPONGE CAKE WITH ANISE LIQUEUR

Rina told me she makes about twenty cakes each month. Which I guess, for a card-carrying rezdora, is just par for the course. Between family and friends, her stand mixer is always going. This particular cake recipe is her version of a sponge cake made with a traditional local anise liqueur called Sassolino. If you can't find Sassolino, don't worry—you can substitute sambuca. SERVES 8 TO 10

1 cup (2 sticks) of unsalted butter, at room temperature

1½ cups of granulated sugar

4 large eggs, at room temperature

Pinch of sea salt

½ cup of Sassolino or other anise liqueur such as sambuca

2 tablespoons of all-purpose flour

2 teaspoons of baking powder

1½ cups of potato starch

Confectioners' sugar, for sprinkling

Preheat the oven 350°F.

Put the butter and sugar in the bowl of a stand mixer and beat until light yellow and fluffy. Add the eggs one at a time, beating well between each egg.

When the mixture is smooth and well incorporated, add the salt, Sassolino, flour, baking powder, and potato starch. Beat until completely blended.

Using a little water, dampen a 12-inch round cake pan and line it with parchment paper. (The dampness helps the parchment stick to the pan.) Pour in the batter and smooth out the top with the back of a spoon. Bake in the oven for 1 hour. Do not open the door while it is cooking, or it will fall. The top should be slightly golden.

Remove from the oven and place on a rack to cool completely. Remove the cake from the pan, place on a cutting board, and sift confectioners' sugar over it to cover.

To serve, using a sharp, large knife, cut the cake into long, 2-inch slices. Then cut them again in the other direction into 2-inch slices to form diamond-shaped pieces. Place the pieces on a platter and serve.

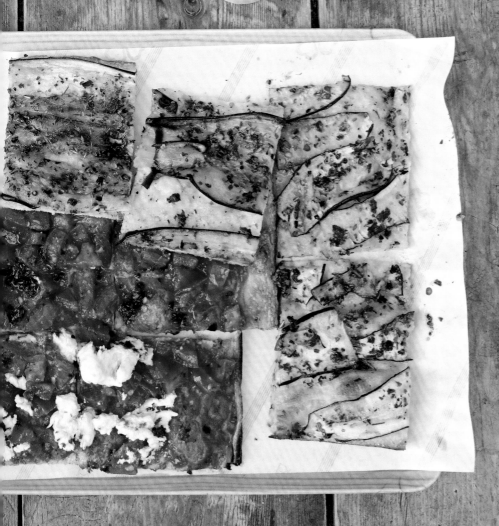

PIZZA BY THE SLICE IN ROME

Even though many people think that pizza originated in Naples, dough topped with tomatoes, cheese, and an infinite number of possible vegetables is made and eaten all over Italy, and has been for centuries. Sometimes the dough is square, other times round. Sometimes the dough is baked in wood-fueled ovens, other times only electric will do. Some are thick and some are thin and the names change as well. In Florence you'll ask for *schiacciata* while in Bari it's *focaccia*.

The customs and traditions surrounding the slice vary as well. Even in Rome, there are three distinct types of pizza to choose from. There are pizzerie that turn out paper-thin single-serving round pizzas from a wood-fired oven. And there are bakeries that make three-foot-long pizzas to sell by the piece and by weight. And then there are the *pizzeria al taglio* places, which are a specific and extremely Roman institution.

Pizza al taglio translates as "pizza by the slice." These small streetfront shops appear all over Rome, and are usually set up more or less the same way. The doors, which are almost always wide open to the street, give way to a small space facing a large, glass-fronted counter. Laid out on the counter, in baking sheets blackened by time and use, are large pan pizzas. Each pan displays a different type of pizza, the choices constantly changing as empty pans are replaced by piping hot pizza-filled pans fresh from the oven. The number of pizzas at any given time is only limited by the width of the store and its counter.

In the meantime, in the back, huge electric ovens—almost all made by Castelli specifically for this purpose—are turning out new pizzas all day long, with a mad crush between noon and 3:00 pm for lunch.

Although some people just order one kind of pizza, the more common approach is to choose a variety. A bit of this, a bit of that. As the customer chooses, the server uses a knife and spatula to cut and grab the slice before setting it on a scale to weigh it. (Prices are per weight, depending on the topping.) Once the various slices have been gathered, they are put onto a small paper-topped tray or cutting board, cut into bite-sized squares, and taken by the customer to a small counter at the side of the shop. If you're lucky there are stools, but it's usually a stand-up-and-eat kind of meal.

In Rome there are pizza al taglio places in every neighborhood. You can always spot the best ones since they usually have a line forming at peak times. Since this type of pizza is never very expensive (except for a few higher-end spots, like Gabriele Bonci's Pizzarium), most of the best places can be found near neighborhoods that have a lot of office workers and/or students.

One of my favorites is the hard-to-find Li Scalini. Located at the end of a dead-end alley not far from Rome's university, it is a traditional pizza al taglio place run by the Messina family. It truly is a mom-and-pop shop, with the father, Massimilliano, in the back making the pizzas while the son, Manuel, is out front serving customers and taking orders.

Several things make Li Scalini one of the better places, and the long-rising dough is a big one. There was a time in Rome when a lot of pizza places began to cut corners, using low-quality ingredients (cheap olive oil, industrially made cheese, etc.) and quick-acting yeasts so that the doughs only took a few hours to rise. This meant that although the dough appeared to be light and fluffy, once eaten it was like a piece of lead in your stomach. Li Scalini is part of a new trend in pizza making, a return to traditional long rising times (twenty-four to forty-eight hours) that put the emphasis on high-quality dough, as it should be. Not only does the time raise the digestibility of the dough, but it also improves the flavor.

Each pizzeria usually has a mixture of some of the classics (marinara, margherita, potato) as well as some signature innovative toppings. But one rule holds true for all of them: there are never more than two or three main toppings on any one pizza.

Recipe for a Party

Since pizza al taglio in Rome is almost always a casual affair, eaten either standing up, perched on a stool, or even while walking, this is the perfect kind of meal to serve as a buffet. Although some of the pizzas are best enjoyed piping hot, others are perfectly fine—or even better—at room temperature.

The dough recipe makes enough for two large pan pizzas, each one measuring 12 by 16 inches. To serve a crowd, it's fun to make a variety of pizzas so that everyone can try a bit of each. You can usually figure on one full dough recipe feeding four to six people. In other words, each full pan feeds two or three. So if you made all of the pizzas on this menu you would have enough for 12 to 18 people. If you are like me, and always err on the side of too much, let me share the pleasures of reheated pizza (with an egg on top) for breakfast.

menu

Pizza all'Insalata
SALAD PIZZA 57

Pizza Margherita
TOMATO AND MOZZARELLA PIZZA 58

Pizza con Melanzane o Zucchine
EGGPLANT OR ZUCCHINI PIZZA 60

Pizza con Prosciutto, Arugula e Pomodorini
PROSCIUTTO, ARUGULA, AND CHERRY TOMATO PIZZA 61

Pizza con Patate e Scamorza Affumicato
POTATO AND SMOKED SCAMORZA PIZZA 64

Piccantina
SPICY PIZZA 65

what to drink

BEER OR SODA

Romans almost never drink wine with pizza. You'll see most people with either a beer or—even more common—a soft drink. I hate to break it to you, but in the center of every table will be a one-liter bottle of soda. Because Italians don't drink soda all the time, the appearance of any carbonated soft drink is thought of as an indulgent treat.

Beer, on the other hand, is thought of less as a form of alcohol and more as something that is truly thirst-quenching. Just what you want with a slice of salty, greasy, cheesy pizza, right?

You can offer some of the classic Italian brands like Chinotto (a citrusy and not-too-sweet cola) or even Aranciata (a carbonated orange-juice drink). And for beer, while you can certainly go the Peroni or Nastro Azzurro route and feel yourself to be 100 percent authentic, some of the smaller Italian craft beers, like Baladin, are now widely available.

timing

1 DAY BEFORE

Make all of the dough and let it rise overnight in the refrigerator. Begin to prepare the dough about 24 hours before you plan to serve dinner.

9 HOURS BEFORE

The morning of your dinner, **remove the dough** from the refrigerator, **fold it** following the directions on page 54, and **place it back in the refrigerator.**

Make the Arugula Oil.

4 HOURS BEFORE

Take the dough out of the refrigerator and **divide it in two** following the directions on page 54. While the dough is doing its final rise **set the table** (see page 52). **Prepare all of the topping ingredients** and place them in small bowls, ready to use.

2½ HOURS BEFORE

Begin to assemble and bake the pizzas according to the recipes, leaving the ones you want to serve warm or hot for last.

Note: Some of the pizza bases can be made ahead of time, to free up oven space for the last-minute pizzas to serve hot. During the party, it's okay to bring out the pizzas one or two at a time; that is how it's done at the pizzerias, with fresh pizzas appearing every ten minutes or so.

The bases for the following pizzas can be made first, then set aside to be topped at the last minute:

Salad Pizza: Prepare the tomato-covered base beforehand, then top with salad when guests have arrived.

Spicy Pizza: Prepare the tomato-covered base beforehand, then either reheat the base and top it with the cherry tomato salad, or just top the cooled pizza base with the tomato salad.

Eggplant or Zucchini Pizza: Prepare ahead of time and either serve at room temperature or reheat it briefly to serve warm.

Pizza with Prosciutto, Arugula, and Cherry Tomatoes: Prepare the tomato base ahead of time and serve at room temperature or reheat it briefly to serve warm.

These two pizzas should be made last minute and served piping hot. If you do make them ahead of time, reheat them thoroughly before serving:

Pizza with Tomatoes and Mozzarella

Pizza with Potatoes and Smoked Scamorza

{continued}

inspiration

SET YOUR TABLE

It's pretty easy to set up your own facsimile of a pizza al taglio shop in Rome. Think of this as a buffet where you are running things from behind your serving table. Set it up so that guests can approach along one side while you serve from the other. If possible, serve each pizza straight out of the pan it was cooked in. This may mean investing in about six pizza pans, but maybe the investment will encourage you to entertain this way more often?

Since you will be setting hot pans on the table, make sure you have some sort of protection between them. I use cork trivets or wooden cutting boards for more stability.

Precut the pizza into little squares or rectangles. Remember to keep the pieces on the small side, so that guests can try more than one kind. Although most pizzerias use a short serrated knife for slicing, I find a pair of kitchen shears leads to fewer tears. Provide small spatulas to lift the pizza from tray to plate.

TABLEWARE AND UTENSILS

Pizza al taglio places never, ever use ceramic plates. Clients are served their pizza on a small cardboard tray with fluted edges, a small wooden pizza board, or—as Pizzeria Li Scalini does—a plastic tray covered with a sheet of paper. Use durable paper napkins. No flatware is needed.

GLASSWARE

For that authentic pizzeria al taglio vibe, use plastic or—more sustainable—paper.

24-Hour Pizza Dough

Everyone has his or her own favorite pizza dough recipe. This one is mine. It does take a long time to rise, but the result is a crust that is light and easy to digest. The problem with doughs that rise too quickly is that even if they taste good, they can be heavy on your stomach. And isn't the goal to be able to eat as many slices as possible?

Don't be put off by the overnight rising. After you do it one or two times, it becomes routine. I usually begin this process the evening before we are going to have pizza for dinner. I make my dough at about 5:00 pm, then it is ready by the next day at 5:00 pm. Time your own dough to start it about 24 hours before your guests are due to arrive. MAKES ENOUGH DOUGH FOR TWO PIZZAS MEASURING 12 BY 16 INCHES

1½ teaspoons of active dry yeast

2½ cups of lukewarm water

2 teaspoons of honey or sugar

About 4 cups of unsifted all-purpose flour, plus more for the work surface

1 tablespoon of sea salt

6 tablespoons of extra-virgin olive oil, plus more for the bowl and baking pans

---

Place the yeast in a small bowl and add about ⅓ cup of the lukewarm water and the honey. Stir to dissolve and let sit for about 10 minutes, until bubbles start to form on the surface of the water.

Prepare a lightly floured work surface and a large, lightly oiled bowl.

Put the flour in another large mixing bowl, and add the salt, stirring to combine it into the flour. Make a well in the center of the flour and pour in the yeast mixture, olive oil, and the remaining water.

Stir, using a wooden spoon at first. When the mixture starts to come together and becomes too difficult to stir, transfer the dough to the lightly floured surface and knead it with your hands. The dough will be pretty sticky at first. Try to avoid adding any more flour, but if you need to add a bit to be able to continue kneading, that's okay.

Knead for 15 to 20 minutes, until the dough is sleek, smooth, and springy to the touch. (Personally, I find kneading to music helps keep me going!)

Form the dough into a ball and place it in the lightly oiled large bowl. Cover with plastic wrap so that no air can get in to dry out the dough. Let the dough sit at room temperature for 30 minutes.

Place the covered bowl in the refrigerator for about 12 hours.

{ *continues* }

Since you began your dough the evening before, the next morning take the dough out of the refrigerator. It should have risen quite a bit (mine usually starts to try to escape the bowl).

Prepare a very lightly floured surface. Take the dough out of the bowl and place it on the surface. Pat the dough down to form a rough rectangle, with a short end nearest you and a long end measuring about 12 inches.

Take the top edge (a short end) in your hands and fold it down two-thirds of the way, just past the center. Repeat with the bottom edge, so that the two edges are now overlapping in the middle, forming a fat, rectangular envelope, with the long side now facing you.

Next, take the right, newly formed short edge, and fold it toward the left, two-thirds of the way, just past the center. Take the left edge and fold it to the right, about two-thirds of the way, overlapping the other edge.

You should now have a "ball" of dough, more or less. Place this ball of dough, seam side down, in the same lightly oiled bowl, covered with plastic wrap. Refrigerate for another 5 hours.

After 5 hours, remove the dough from the refrigerator. Divide the dough into two pieces.

Repeat the folding process described previously for each of the pieces. Then place the balls of dough on a lightly oiled tray, cover with a clean cloth, and let rise until doubled in bulk. This will take a couple of hours.

When you are ready to bake the pizzas, preheat the oven to 450°F. Coat the bottom, but not the sides, of the baking pans with olive oil.

Prepare a lightly floured surface and gently turn a ball of dough out onto it, seam side down. Using your fingers, gently poke the dough from the center outward, slowly forming a rough rectangle (or at least an oval). Try not to

flatten the dough too much. You are trying to maintain as many air bubbles as possible that may have formed while rising. When the dough is 1 to 2 inches smaller than the size of your pan, transfer it to the pan by using your clean hand to flip the top half of the pizza over your other clean forearm. (This avoids stretching the dough with your hand and/or fingers to the point of breaking.) Gently stretch the dough so that it comes to the edges of the pan, pinching it to the sides.

Proceed with the type of pizza you are making, according to the following recipes. For all options, keep in mind that all ovens are different, so timing is approximate. You'll get the hang of how your oven treats the pizzas the more you make them.

GENERAL NOTE FOR PIZZA RECIPES At a certain point—either before or after baking—most of these recipes call for seasoning the pizza with salt and drizzling it with olive oil. Use a pretty heavy hand, especially with the olive oil.

If you find yourself with leftover dough, you can freeze it. Wrap it up tightly in plastic wrap, or place it in a ziptop bag. Before using the frozen dough, place it in the refrigerator to thaw out overnight and then bring to room temperature. Another option is to simply bake an extra pizza bianca (olive oil–topped pizza) to eat the next day or else freeze in pieces already cooked. You can just pop a slice of pizza bianca directly into the toaster to thaw out and then eat, much like you would a frozen bagel half.

Olio di Rughetta

ARUGULA OIL

This is the magic ingredient I learned from my friends at Pizzeria Li Scalini. While I was hanging out in the kitchen, I saw that the final touch was a bright green liquid drizzled over the toppings with a spoon, providing a vivid, verdant touch to the finished pie. "If a pizza doesn't look attractive, no one wants to eat it," Massimiliano explained. So every morning they whip up a batch of arugula oil, chopping a few big bunches of fresh, spicy arugula, then spinning it in the blender with extra-virgin olive oil. A squeeze of this atop the pizza, rather than just plain olive oil, not only provides eye candy, but also has the fresh bite of the peppery greens.

This quickly made oil should be applied at the last minute, right before the pizza goes to the table. **MAKES ABOUT 1 CUP**

1 bunch of arugula, rinsed and dried

½ cup or more of extra-virgin olive oil

Put the arugula in a food processor. With the blade running on high, slowly drizzle in the olive oil. When it is a smooth, bright green puree, transfer it into a small bowl. If not using right away, cover it with plastic wrap and place it in the refrigerator. Although it won't go bad for a few days, the bite of the arugula tends to wear off, so it's best to use it within 24 hours.

Pizza all'Insalata

SALAD PIZZA

When you can't decide between a salad and pizza, this recipe is for you. It's another pizza that you can make ahead of time, with a room-temperature topping. If you can get fresh corn, then all the better. But really? Canned corn and balsamic do provide that authentic Roman pizza al taglio flavor. The combination offers a sweet element like the kind you find on absolutely inauthentic pizza with pineapple in the USA.

Every pizzeria has its own version of what they put on top. My favorite harks back to the one I used to get in the Jewish Ghetto on the way to school in the morning. I called it Salad Pizza. I figured that the slightly pickled artichokes and slices of hard-boiled egg made it an appropriate breakfast food. **SERVES 2 OR 3**

Two 14-ounce cans of crushed tomatoes

1 tablespoon of extra-virgin olive oil, plus more for the pan and for drizzling

½ recipe of 24-Hour Pizza Dough (page 53)

Sea salt and freshly ground black pepper

4 cups of mixed salad greens

1 teaspoon of red wine vinegar

One 6-ounce can of tuna packed in olive oil

½ cup of fresh corn kernels, boiled, or drained canned corn

½ cup of drained sliced jarred artichoke hearts

2 hard-boiled eggs, thinly sliced

Aceto Balsamico di Modena or regular red wine vinegar mixed with a bit of honey

Arugula Oil (opposite)

Pour the tomatoes into a sieve over a bowl and let them drain for a half hour at room temperature.

Preheat the oven to 450°F. Lightly oil the bottom of a 12 by 16-inch rectangular pizza pan.

Roll out the dough and transfer it to the pan as per the instructions on page 55. Spread a thin layer of the drained tomatoes over the top, leaving a ½-inch rim of dough around the edge. Don't overdo it. Season to taste with salt and drizzle with olive oil.

Bake for 20 minutes, until the crust begins to turn golden and the topping is sizzling. Remove from the oven and let cool to room temperature.

Just before you are ready to serve the pizza, place the salad greens in a bowl and dress them lightly with 1 tablespoon olive oil, the red wine vinegar, and salt and pepper to taste (as if you were dressing a salad). Evenly scatter the salad over the pizza.

Open and drain the can of tuna, then scatter it over the pizza, followed by the corn, artichokes, and eggs. Drizzle with Aceto Balsamico di Modena and arugula oil. Serve immediately.

Pizza Margherita

TOMATO AND MOZZARELLA PIZZA

Even though pizza makers all over Rome try their hand at inventive toppings, if you ask any of them which is their most requested type of pizza, the answer is always Margherita. This classic—tomatoes, mozzarella, and basil—is everyone's favorite. SERVES 2 OR 3

9 ounces of fresh mozzarella

Two 14-ounce cans of crushed tomatoes

Extra-virgin olive oil

½ recipe of 24-Hour Pizza Dough (page 53)

Sea salt

Torn fresh basil leaves

Using your hands, rip the mozzarella into small pieces and place it in a sieve. Let it drain over a bowl for an hour at room temperature.

Pour the tomatoes into a sieve over a separate bowl and let them drain for a half hour at room temperature.

Preheat the oven to 450°F. Lightly oil the bottom of a 12 by 16-inch rectangular pizza pan.

Roll out the dough and transfer it to the pan as per the instructions on page 55. Spread a layer of the drained tomatoes on top. Don't overdo it. (Don't worry if you have some tomatoes left over. You can freeze them and use them in your next batch of sauce.) Season to taste with salt and olive oil.

Bake for 15 minutes, until the crust starts to turn golden and the topping is bubbling.

Remove the pizza from the oven and scatter the mozzarella over the top, leaving an inch or more of space between pieces.

Place the pizza back in the oven for another 5 minutes, allowing the mozzarella to melt. You don't want the cheese to brown, just to become runny.

Remove from the oven, drizzle with more olive oil, and top with the basil leaves. Serve immediately.

Pizza con Melanzane o Zucchine

EGGPLANT OR ZUCCHINI PIZZA

This is basically a vegetarian pizza if you skip the prosciutto, and it can also
be vegan, if you forgo the prosciutto and cheeses. These days a lot of people don't
want a heavy, ingredient-laden slice of pizza in the middle of the day, and this is
Li Scalini's answer. If you want to make it a bit more substantial, though, it's easy
to add on slices of Prosciutto di Parma or torn fresh mozzarella after the pizza has
cooked. I like topping the pizza with grated pecorino and putting it back in the oven
for 5 minutes, until the cheese melts and starts to turn golden. It's great with arugula
oil on top. SERVES 2 OR 3

(pictured pages 46–47; page 62, top left)

**2 small eggplants, sliced into ⅛- to
¼-inch rounds**

**2 medium zucchini, sliced lengthwise ⅛ to
¼ inch thick**

Sea salt

Two 14-ounce cans of crushed tomatoes

Extra-virgin olive oil

½ recipe of 24-Hour Pizza Dough (page 53)

1 to 2 teaspoons of fresh or dried oregano

6 slices of Prosciutto di Parma (optional)

1 cup of torn fresh mozzarella (optional)

**Up to 8 ounces of pecorino cheese, grated
(2 cups; optional)**

Arugula Oil (page 56; optional)

Sprinkle the eggplant and zucchini lightly with
salt and let them drain for a half hour in a
colander. Pat dry completely with paper towels.

Pour the tomatoes into a sieve over a bowl
and let them drain for a half hour at room
temperature.

Preheat the oven to 450°F. Lightly oil the bottom
of a 12 by 16-inch rectangular pizza.

Roll out the dough and transfer it to the pan as
per the instructions on page 55. Spread a layer
of the drained tomatoes on top. Don't overdo
it. Season with salt and drizzle with olive oil to
taste. Lay the eggplant over one half of the pizza,
and the zucchini over the other half. Drizzle
with more olive oil and season to taste with
more salt and oregano.

Bake for 20 minutes, until the dough begins
to turn golden and the topping is sizzling.
Remove from the oven and let the pizza cool to
room temperature. Top it with the prosciutto,
mozzarella, pecorino, and/or arugula oil, if
using. If adding pecorino, you can run it under
the broiler for a minute or two.

Pizza con Prosciutto, Arugula e Pomodorini

PROSCIUTTO, ARUGULA, AND CHERRY TOMATO PIZZA

A version of salad pizza but a bit meatier, this recipe calls for Prosciutto di Parma, but feel free to substitute bresaola or even sliced turkey. Since so much of the success of this pizza depends on cherry tomatoes, use the best ones you can find. And if it's the dead of winter? Then better to double the amount of fresh arugula and forget about the cherry tomatoes. **SERVES 2 OR 3**

(pictured page 62, bottom left)

Two 14-ounce cans of crushed tomatoes

Extra-virgin olive oil

½ recipe of 24-Hour Pizza Dough (page 53)

Sea salt

4 cups of arugula, rinsed and dried

2 cups of quartered cherry tomatoes

9 ounces of thinly sliced Prosciutto di Parma or other cured meat

Arugula Oil (page 56)

Pour the crushed tomatoes into a sieve over a bowl and let them drain for a half hour at room temperature.

Preheat the oven to 450°F. Lightly oil the bottom of a 12 by 16-inch rectangular pizza pan.

Roll out the dough and transfer it to the pan as per the instructions on page 55. Spread a layer of the drained tomatoes on top. Don't overdo it. Season to taste with salt and drizzle with olive oil.

Bake for 20 minutes, until the crust begins to turn golden and the topping is sizzling. Remove from the oven and let cool to room temperature.

Just before you are ready to serve the pizza, place the arugula in a bowl with the cherry tomatoes and dress lightly with olive oil and salt. Lay the prosciutto on top of the pizza, then evenly scatter the salad over the pizza. Drizzle with the arugula oil. Serve immediately.

Pizza con Patate e Scarmorza Affumicato

POTATO AND SMOKED SCAMORZA PIZZA

Pizza con patate (pizza with potatoes) is one of my favorite slices in Rome. Often made with just potatoes and no cheese, it's what I usually grab from the bakery in Campo de' Fiori for a midmorning snack. But this version with smoked scamorza, made at Li Scalini, is just as good, and a bit more of a real meal. Scamorza is mozzarella's older sibling, a cow's milk cheese made in the same way as mozzarella, but drained and aged a bit, and—in this case—lightly smoked. **SERVES 2 OR 3**

(pictured page 62, bottom right)

4 medium potatoes

1 tablespoon of extra-virgin olive oil, plus more for the pan and drizzling

½ recipe of 24-Hour Pizza Dough (page 53)

9 ounces of smoked scamorza, torn

¼ cup of fresh rosemary leaves

Sea salt

Peel the potatoes and slice them very thinly, into about ⅛-inch-thick slices. (A mandoline works well, if you have one.) Put the slices in a microwave-safe dish and coat them with the olive oil. Place in the microwave and cook on high for 2 minutes. Take the potatoes out, stir them, and put them back in for another 2 minutes. Take them out and taste; they should be tender, but firm.

Preheat the oven to 450°F. Lightly oil the bottom of a 12 by 16-inch rectangular pizza pan.

Roll out the dough and transfer it to the pan as per the instructions on page 55. Cover the dough with the potatoes, leaving a ½-inch rim around the edge. Scatter the cheese, and then the rosemary leaves, on top. Drizzle with olive oil and season with salt to taste. Brush some olive oil along the rim of the pizza.

Bake for 20 minutes, or until the crust begins to turn golden and the cheese bubbles. Serve immediately.

Piccantina

SPICY PIZZA

This pizza is one of my favorites, and you'll find versions of it all over Rome. The good thing about making this pizza at home is that it can be partially prepared ahead of time: you can bake the tomato-covered base beforehand, then either heat it up before topping it with the raw ingredients or just top the room-temperature pizza, which is what they do in the pizzeria. The name, Piccantina, comes from the word *piccante*, which means spicy. Use more or fewer red pepper flakes according to how piccante you like your pizza. **SERVES 2 OR 3**

(pictured page 63, bottom)

Two 14-ounce cans of crushed tomatoes

2 tablespoons of extra-virgin olive oil, plus more for the pan and for drizzling

½ recipe of 24-Hour Pizza Dough (page 53)

Sea salt

1 teaspoon of red pepper flakes, or to taste

3 cups of halved or quartered cherry tomatoes

1 cup of pitted briny black olives

2 teaspoons of dried oregano

Arugula Oil (page 56)

Pour the crushed tomatoes into a sieve over a bowl and let them drain for a half hour at room temperature.

Preheat the oven to 450°F. Lightly oil the bottom of a 12 by 16-inch rectangular pizza pan.

Roll out the dough and transfer it to the pan as per the instructions on page 55. Spread a thin layer of the drained tomatoes over the top, leaving a ½-inch rim around the edges. Don't overdo it. Season to taste with salt and red pepper flakes, and drizzle with olive oil.

Bake for 20 minutes, or until the crust begins to turn golden and the topping is sizzling. Remove from the oven and let cool to room temperature.

Just before you are ready to serve the pizza, you can either reheat the base for 5 minutes in a 450°F oven or proceed with the base at room temperature. Toss the cherry tomatoes with 2 tablespoons olive oil and 1 teaspoon salt. Mix to coat well and spread over the top of the pizza. Scatter with the olives and oregano and drizzle with arugula oil.

PORCHETTA PICNIC IN ARICCIA

If you've traveled through central Italy—in Tuscany, Umbria, and Lazio—then you may have seen trailers parked by the side of the road. Awnings shade a line of customers whose numbers increase around lunchtime. This is the porchetta truck, which is pretty much the mother of all food trucks. They sell one thing, and one thing only: thick slices of fragrant, fatty, crispy roast porchetta.

Porchetta, in case you've never had the pleasure of encountering one, is an entire pig that has been deboned, seasoned, and roasted for up to twenty hours. The result is fatty, savory, tender meat on the inside, and crisp, crackling skin on the outside. This dish is made throughout Italy, and naturally, each region has its own customs and variations. In Abruzzo it is served warm out of the oven; in Umbria, the liver is used for the stuffing and the entire thing is only eaten once it has cooled off. In Sardegna, *porceduu* is a small suckling pig roasted with myrtle leaves that's always pulled apart and eaten with your hands.

The epicenter of porchetta is generally considered to be Ariccia, about thirty minutes south of Rome, in the Frascati hills. This town is known for its glistening, massive porchetta. The animals are deboned, but the legs and head are left attached. The meat is then seasoned with rosemary, sage, garlic, salt, and pepper. Once cooked by the family-owned businesses around town, the finished roasts can weigh anywhere from thirty to ninety pounds. They are then shipped out to truck stands as well as *alimentari* (delis) and other vendors throughout Italy.

Of course, the best place to indulge is in Ariccia itself, home to several distinct and traditional ways to enjoy it. The easiest is to stop by one of the stands, where the vendor will slice open a crusty roll and fill your sandwich according to your personal taste: within that huge hunk-o'-meat you might prefer fatty over lean (well, relatively lean) or extra bits of the crisp skin. And there are sure to be *nonne* or housewives lining up as well, ready to bring home a tray of freshly cut slices for lunch or dinner.

But the all-time most fun, best, and most delicious way to enjoy porchetta in Ariccia is as part of a multicourse meal that takes place in a type of local restaurant known as a *fraschetta*.

The word *fraschetta* comes from *frasca*, which means "leafy branch." For centuries small wine shops selling the local wine from the surrounding Frascati hills would set up rough wooden tables outside their doorways, where pitchers of inexpensive vino would flow freely. To provide shade during the heat of the day, makeshift pergolas were constructed out of *frasche*, or branches. Since there was only wine, people would bring along their own food. Eventually, though, some of the wine shops began to serve simple food: baskets of bread, sheep's milk cheese, prosciutto and sausage and, of course, porchetta. At the beginning there were no real menus, but over the years many shops began to serve cooked food as well, including beans, pasta, and grilled meat, eventually turning into the real restaurants that are known today as *fraschette*.

There are countless fraschette in Ariccia nowadays, located in the town and the surrounding countryside. Romans make the short drive south to have lunch or dinner there, at one of the rough wooden tables groaning under the weight of abundant meals for a very low price. One holdover from the original: huge pitchers of local wine.

Over the years my family and I have been to many these places. One of our favorites, mostly for its location, is La Selva. Located just outside of town, about fifty wooden picnic tables are scattered beneath the shade of massive oak trees. During summer nights, when the coolness of this wooded area provides respite from the heat of nearby Rome, every table is full and the waiters run from one to the next, bringing food and—more importantly—those pitchers of local wine. And because the wine flows so freely, and is almost the same price as water, dining at a fraschetta always feels like a party. While my daughter Sophie tends to head to Ariccia after dark, my preferred time is to escape with my husband, Domenico, for a quiet lunch. The atmosphere is more subdued then, and the place is filled with workers, businessmen, and—not surprisingly—other couples like us, looking for a bucolic (and pork-filled) escape.

Whether you come in the day or the evening, the routine is always the same. As soon as you are seated, the waiter will come over, hastily top the table with a sheet of paper, scatter a handful of forks and knives in the center, and ask two very important questions: "Red or white?" And: *"Cominciamo con antipasti?"* ("Shall we start with antipasti?")

One hundred percent of the diners start with—and never go beyond—antipasti. Once you say yes, the plates start flying out of the kitchen and seemingly don't stop until you've long since unbuttoned your jeans.

While each fraschetta has its own specialty, when it comes to antipasti, some things are givens. There are always cured meats: prosciutto, sausages, and a type of dried pork jerky known as *coppiette*. Cheese is ever-present: mozzarella, of course, but also two or three types of sheep's milk pecorino. Bread comes sliced in a basket, but more is also toasted, rubbed with garlic, and doused with olive oil as bruschetta.

But naturally the main event, which pretty much defines fraschetta dining, is a big plate of porchetta.

The following menu takes its cue from a typical fraschetta meal. I've eliminated pasta mostly because I never get that far. And I think the antipasto-only meal is more relaxed for entertaining. Take my word for it: no one will go hungry. The one thing I have changed is the porchetta element. True porchetta involves deboning and cooking an entire pig. Unless you're planning a wedding, I doubt your party will supply enough hungry guests to finish off sixty pounds of meat. So I'm sharing my own version of faux porchetta. Don't worry, it's pig a-plenty, with as much fat and crispy skin as would show up at your table in Ariccia.

Recipe for a Party

This menu is typical for a night out at a fraschetta in Ariccia, composed of a mixture of cold and cooked dishes. For those with a yard and a picnic table, this is food meant to be served atop a rough wooden table. If you don't have your own backyard, everything in this menu is portable, and you can head to your nearest park and grab a picnic table.

You can also host an indoor fraschetta buffet party. Lay out all the food on big platters, and people can help themselves. This can be as casual as a cocktail party or, if you include all of the dishes, there is enough food to create a real dinner. You can divide the courses like this: *antipasti* (cheeses, cured meats, eggplant, and bruschetta); *secondo* (porchetta, and beans and sausages); *dolce* (wine biscotti).

menu

{*Pane*—Crusty Italian Bread}

Formaggi e Affettati
CHEESES AND CURED MEATS 72

Bruschetta 75

{*Olive Verde*—Green Olives}

Melanzane sott'Olio
MARINATED EGGPLANT 76

Fagioli con le Cotiche
BEANS WITH PORK RIND 78

Salsicette al Vino con Olive
SAUSAGES WITH WINE AND OLIVES 81

Porchetta 82

Dolce

Ciambelline al Vino
WINE BISCOTTI 85

what to drink

WINE

Although the Frascati area is known for its white wines (and some of them are quite good these days) most people order pitchers of Romanella at a fraschetta. Romanella is typical "farmer" wine, a red that is consumed within twelve months. It is somewhat sweet, slightly fizzy, and low in alcohol. Together these characteristics make it perfect for washing down fatty cured meats and porchetta. In the absence of your local farmer supplying you with a barrel of wine, ask your wine store to recommend a low-alcohol red that is, if possible, slightly fizzy. No need to spend much.

timing

Almost everything on this menu can, and should, be prepared ahead of time. Some of the dishes, like the beans and the eggplant, actually improve with time.

2 DAYS BEFORE

Soak the beans. Make the biscotti. Make and marinate the eggplant. Season the porchetta and let it marinate with the rub in the refrigerator.

1 DAY BEFORE

Cook the following dishes: Beans with Pork Rind; Sausages with Wine and Olives; Porchetta.

2 HOURS BEFORE

Take everything out of the refrigerator at least 2 hours before you will be serving the food. While most of the dishes can be eaten at room temperature, you can reheat the beans and the sausages to warm them a bit more if desired.

1 HOUR BEFORE

Prepare the bruschetta topping, but do not toast and serve the bruschette until you are about to sit down. Wait to cut the cheeses and cured meats until 45 minutes before you will be eating them.

inspiration

SET YOUR TABLE

This is picnic table and bench time, whether you're inside or out. But if you are tied to your traditional dining table, there are a few ways you can make it more fraschetta-friendly.

DRESSING YOUR TABLE

This is no time for fancy. In Ariccia the rough wooden tables are covered with sheets of paper, usually ripped off a roll hanging on the wall. If you can find a sheet of paper that will cover your table, fantastic. Alternatively, a plain white disposable tablecloth will serve nicely. The cheapest one you can find, please.

TABLEWARE AND UTENSILS

Most fraschette serve food in one of two ways.

Plastic plates: Different items are placed on individual, no-nonsense disposable plastic plates and plopped in the middle of the table, to be passed around. Wicker tray: Some fraschette do away with serving plates altogether and simply line a rimmed wicker tray with butcher paper and then pile the food on that. (A regular tray will also do.)

Plates and napkins are always disposable. Feel free to substitute more sustainable paper plates. It's important to use thick paper napkins since these foods can be greasy.

Flatware is metal, but cheap. Plastic-handled metal knives are lightweight, cut food well, and are so cheap you won't cry if one goes missing on a picnic.

GLASSWARE

The wine is always the house variety and arrives at the table in an unlabeled bottle or simply in a heavy glass pitcher. Such rustic wine is meant for rustic glasses. Use chunky glass tumblers: one per person, so everyone can either alternate between wine and water or—as many do— dilute their wine with water!

Formaggi e Affettati
CHEESES AND CURED MEATS

Mixed cheeses and cured meats are always part of any antipasto in Ariccia. You can pick and choose what you'd like to serve, but here are a few suggestions to help you get started. Serve three kinds of aged pecorino cheese, three varieties of cured meats, and mozzarella and ricotta.

cheeses

Pecorino: Pecorino is local sheep's milk cheese, and should not be confused with pecorino Romano, which is a hard grating cheese meant to be served atop pasta. If you can't find pecorino from Lazio, don't worry, just look for something from Tuscany (Pienza specifically) or else Sardegna. Try to get at least two different types, one younger and one more aged. There are also semiaged pecorinos flecked with red pepper that are excellent.

Pecorino is always served precut in small pieces (around ¼ inch thick). Traditionally it is served with the rind on, and diners remove the rind from each little piece before eating.

Mozzarella: A glistening wet ball of fresh mozzarella is always a part of this menu. Do not slice the mozzarella, or it will start to lose the liquid from its center. Simply place the ball on a plate and let your guests cut into it at the table.

Ricotta: In Italy fresh sheep's or cow's milk ricotta often comes in small, single-portion baskets. These are turned out onto a plate and drizzled with honey. Don't worry if you can't find the small baskets, just gently lay a wedge or a few spoonfuls (if your ricotta is very soft) on a plate, and top with the honey of your choice.

cured meats

Antipasto in Ariccia is a meatfest, especially cured meats. Feel free to pick and choose, but the following are almost always part of the menu.

Corallo: This is the name for the most common type of dried salami served in Rome and in the countryside around the city. Flavored with whole black peppercorns and flecked with big chunks of white fat, it is a basic type of salami, and very porky. It is fairly mild tasting. If you can't find Roman-style corallo, substitute any type of hard Italian salami.

Salame piccante: This comes in different sizes, but is always distinguished by its red hue thanks to the addition of red pepper, which makes this salami very spicy. It is more commonly called pepperoni in the USA.

{ *continues* }

Salsiciette: These 3-inch-long sausages are usually dark in color and very rustic; the consistency is not fine and smooth, but rough. They can be flavored with fennel seeds and sometimes include wild boar meat.

Prosciutto: Prosciutto appears at every fraschetta meal. The most common type is locally produced and cut by hand into rough slices. Prosciutto di Parma, cut into paper-thin slices will do just fine.

Coppiette: These long strips of lean pork are flavored with fennel seeds and red pepper, and air-dried until cured. This Italian form of pork jerky is cut into bite-sized, chewy bits and served as part of the antipasto.

quantities

In general, since this is a multicourse meal, plan on buying about three ounces of each type of cheese or cured meat per person.

Bruschetta

Even if slices of a big loaf of crusty bread arrive at the table at every fraschetta, even more bread comes in the form of bruschette. Slices of bread are toasted (usually and ideally over a grill), then rubbed with garlic and doused in olive oil. The final touch is a flurry of salt. When tomatoes are in season, those get piled on as well.

A rustic loaf of bread is the main ingredient in this dish—and the hardest part of this recipe. A firm, brittle crust is a must, but also try to get a loaf that is not too full of air bubbles. The bubbles should be evenly distributed, resulting in a firm, dense crumb that will allow the final bruschetta to hold up well to the tomato topping or even just olive oil.   SERVES 6

1 pound of ripe plum tomatoes (see Notes)

1½ teaspoons of sea salt, plus more to taste

2 tablespoons of extra-virgin olive oil, plus more for drizzling

½ cup of fresh basil leaves

6 slices of rustic Italian bread, each ½ inch thick

2 cloves of garlic, peeled

Prepare the grill if using.

Chop the tomatoes into bite-sized pieces, about ½ inch or so. (You should have 3 cups.) Put them in a small bowl and add the salt, olive oil, and basil leaves. Stir well but gently. Let the mixture sit for at least 20 minutes to allow the juices to develop.

Grill the bread if possible, or toast it in a toaster or your oven (see Notes). The bread should be toasted but not burnt. When grilling, it's very easy to get distracted and burn your bread. Be vigilant!

While the bread is still hot, rub one side of each slice with garlic, being careful not to burn your fingers. Place the bread on a serving platter, drizzle olive oil on top, and sprinkle with salt. Top with the tomatoes, dividing them between the bruschetta. Let them sit for 5 minutes so the bread can absorb the juices, then serve.

NOTES If it's not tomato season, then it's best to simply skip the tomatoes. In fact, most fraschette in Ariccia serve bruschetta "naked" with just garlic, olive oil, and salt.

Do not oil the bread before you toast it. Bruschetta is *never* oiled first.

Melanzane sott'Olio

MARINATED EGGPLANT

At least one little plate full of *sott'oli* always comes to the table at a fraschetta. Sott'oli are vegetables—usually summer ones—that have been preserved by first blanching them in a vinegar-water mix or grilling them briefly and then preserving them in seasoned olive oil. My favorite kind is made with eggplant. Sometimes the eggplants are grilled first (as in Campania), sometimes they are raw (as is common in Puglia), but by the time you eat them, they have always been marinating in the olive oil for at least a month while the flavors blend and the eggplant cures. When I can't wait that long, I use this speedy version. Not only is it faster (and involves no canning skills!) but it's just a tad bit lighter, too.

Although I've included this recipe for homemade marinated eggplant, feel free to just open up a few jars of preserved vegetables from your local Italian grocer instead or in addition. Marinated peppers, artichokes, giardiniera (a mix of pickled vegetables), and sun-dried tomatoes preserved in olive oil are good choices. And olives. Don't forget olives! SERVES 4 OR 5

⅓ cup of white wine vinegar

1 teaspoon of dried oregano

3 cloves of garlic, peeled

½ cup of extra-virgin olive oil

1 teaspoon of sea salt

½ teaspoon of freshly ground black pepper

1½ pounds of firm eggplants

1 or 2 fresh Italian chile peppers, sliced

1 small bunch of Italian flat-leaf parsley, chopped (optional)

Preheat the broiler to its highest setting. Place an oven rack about 3 inches away from the broiler element.

To make the marinade: Pour the vinegar into a small glass bowl and add the oregano. Grate the garlic using a Microplane, or use a garlic press, and stir the crushed garlic into the marinade. Let it sit for at least 30 minutes.

In another small bowl mix the olive oil, salt, and pepper.

Cut the stems off of the eggplants and slice them into ¼-inch rounds. Brush each side of the rounds with some of the olive oil mixture and place them on a rack over a baking sheet. The eggplant should be in one layer, so you will probably have to do this in two batches.

Place the baking sheet under the broiler. Let the eggplant slices cook for 6 minutes, then turn them over and cook for 4 minutes more. Be careful not to let them burn.

While the eggplant slices are still hot, place them in an 8 by 10-inch shallow glass dish, layering them on top of one another. Using a spoon, drizzle the marinade on top of each layer, as well as some of the sliced chile peppers.

Cover the dish with plastic wrap and let marinate in the refrigerator for at least 24 hours.

Take it out of the refrigerator 1 hour before serving. Serve at room temperature, with the parsley sprinkled over, if using.

Fagioli con le Cotiche
BEANS WITH PORK RIND

This simple bean dish is a good example of *cucina povera*, or peasant cooking. It takes an inexpensive ingredient—dried beans—and flavors it with just a bit of a cut of meat that often gets thrown away: pork rind (*cotiche*). Fagioli con le cotiche can feature more or less rind, depending on whether it is being served as a side dish (as on this menu) or a main dish. In this version, just a bit of cotiche adds a lot of flavor. Although your supermarket may not carry pork rind, you should be able to find it, or at least order it, from a butcher. I usually have him scrape away the extra layer of fat from the inside.

This recipe depends on good-quality dried beans, not canned, so you need to remember to start soaking them the night before you plan on cooking them. They can even be cooked the day before you finish making the dish.

Don't be put off by all the separate steps to this recipe. None of them are in any way complicated. And while you can serve this dish immediately after making it, it's even better reheated the next day. **SERVES 6 TO 8**

½ **pound of dried cannellini beans**

1 **teaspoon of sea salt**

1 **medium carrot, peeled**

1 **large onion, cut in half**

6 **ounces of pork rind**

½ **stalk of celery**

For the tomato sauce

5 **tablespoons of extra-virgin olive oil**

¼ **cup of chopped yellow onion**

2 **cloves of garlic, chopped**

½ **teaspoon of sea salt**

⅛ **to ¼ teaspoon of red pepper flakes**

⅓ **cup of chopped fresh Italian flat-leaf parsley**

2 **cups of tomato puree**

The night before you're going to cook this dish, place the dried beans in a bowl and cover with water. Let them soak for at least 12 hours.

Drain and rinse the beans and put them in a large pot. Cover them with water by 2 inches.

Bring the beans to a slow simmer over low heat. Using a spoon, skim off the foam that appears at the surface. Once the foam stops forming, add the salt, the carrot, and one half of the onion. Place the lid on the pot halfway, and let the beans simmer until tender. This can take anywhere from 40 minutes to 1½ hours, depending on how old your beans are. Don't let them get too mushy. They don't need stirring, but do use a spoon to taste a bean every so often for doneness.

When the beans are tender, drain them. Remove and discard the onion and carrot.

In the meantime, cook the pork rind: Bring a large pot of water (about 6 cups) to a boil. Place the rind in the pot and cook for 20 minutes.

Drain and transfer the rind to a cutting board, reserving the cooking water. Using a sharp knife, cut the rind into ¼-inch strips, and then cut the strips into 2-inch lengths. Refill the pot with water and bring to a simmer. Place the strips in the water along with the celery and the remaining onion half. Simmer until tender, 45 minutes to an hour. (The rind will still be chewy.) Drain, reserving the cooking water but discarding the celery and onion.

To make the sauce: Pour the olive oil into a pot large enough to eventually hold all the ingredients (the beans, sauce, and the rind) and add the chopped onion, garlic, salt, and red pepper flakes to taste. Simmer over medium heat until the onion is tender, about 8 minutes. Add the parsley and stir, then add the tomato puree. Let the sauce cook until it has a reduced a bit, about 20 minutes.

Add the beans and rind to the sauce and stir. Add about ¾ cup of the rind cooking water. Let the beans and rind cook for about 30 minutes, adding more cooking water if it seems too dried out. At this point everything is already cooked through, and you are just cooking for the final half hour to bring all of the flavors together. Serve immediately, or let the flavors blend for a day before reheating and serving.

Salsicette al Vino con Olive

SAUSAGES WITH WINE AND OLIVES

Every fraschetta has a few signature dishes. While this standout mixture of sausage and olives is one of my favorites, I can't remember exactly where I enjoyed it. (Too much of that Romanella wine?) In any case, it's a great part of an antipasto buffet, but also can stand on its own as a main dish. To serve it as part of the buffet, cut the sausages into halves or thirds (bite-sized pieces) once they are cooked, to make them easier to eat by the forkful. (*Salsicette* means "little sausage.") SERVES 4 OR 5

3 tablespoons of extra-virgin olive oil

1 pound of not-too-spicy fresh Italian-style sausages (about 8)

½ cup of chopped white onion

½ teaspoon of sea salt

½ teaspoon of fennel seeds

1½ cups of big green unpitted olives

1 cup of dry white wine

Pour the olive oil into a 10- or 12-inch frying pan and set over medium heat.

Using a fork or a sharp knife, poke holes all over the sausages (this will let the fat drain out, and make sure the sausages don't burst while cooking), and place them in the pan with the olive oil. Brown well, turning to make sure you get all the sides. This should take about 10 minutes. Once browned, transfer the sausages to a plate.

If the sausages have given up a lot of fat, remove all but 1 tablespoon from the pan, but be careful to leave the browned bits in the pan. Add the onions to the fat, reducing the heat to medium-low. Add the salt, and using a wooden spoon, stir the onions, scraping up the browned bits at the bottom of the pan. Cook the onions until tender, about 8 minutes, but do not let them brown.

Add the fennel seeds and cook a few more minutes. Return the sausages to the pan and add the olives and wine. Bring to a simmer and cook, covered, for 10 minutes, stirring once or twice. Uncover the pan and cook off any leftover wine.

Serve the olives and sausages warm or at room temperature. If serving as part of a stand-up buffet, then cut each sausage into smaller pieces before placing them on a serving platter or in a bowl.

Porchetta

In the introduction I sang the praises of porchetta done the traditional way. Making it that way at home is usually not an option since a) not many people host the crowds necessary to devour an entire pig and b) even if you did, you probably don't have an oven big enough.

The following recipe is my home version. A true porchetta contains the loin as well as the belly (pictured page 84, right), but this recipe is pure belly. This not only ensures a tender, tasty outcome, but it also means that the entire roast will be cooked through, without any part drying out.

When ordering the pork belly, make sure to tell your butcher you would like yours with the rind on, please. And if you can get him to score the rind in a diamond pattern, all the better. If not, you can try to do so yourself, though it's not easy. If that doesn't work, jab yours with the point of your knife to make some holes. However you accomplish this part, it is essential, since it allows the fat to leak out during cooking, turning it into crisp crackling. The pork belly needs to marinate for a day before cooking and then it takes about seven hours to complete the process, so be sure to leave yourself plenty of time. In most parts of Italy porchetta is served cool or at room temperature. So if you can let it cool off completely, or cool it and serve it the next day, even better. **SERVES 8 TO 10**

---

7 pounds of pork belly, in 1 piece, with rind attached

1 cup of fresh sage leaves

1 cup of rosemary leaves

6 cloves of garlic, peeled

1 tablespoon of fennel seeds

Grated zest from 1 organic, unsprayed lemon (if using a conventional lemon, scrub it well and dry it)

1 tablespoon of sea salt

1 teaspoon of freshly ground black pepper, plus more to taste

5 tablespoons of extra-virgin olive oil

Wash and pat dry the pork belly. Lay it on a flat surface, with the rind up. If the butcher has not scored the rind, try to do so yourself or use a very sharp knife to poke a lot of holes in the rind.

Put the sage, rosemary, garlic, fennel seeds, lemon zest, salt, pepper, and olive oil in a food processor and process until finely chopped.

Flip the pork belly over so the inside is up. Rub about half of the paste over the meat. Roll the roast up as tightly as you can, from the long end. Using a long piece of twine, secure it evenly along the entire length of the roast, looping it around every few inches. If you've never done

this before, you may need someone else to help hold it together while you're tying it.

Rub the rest of the seasoning all over the outside and both ends, and push some into the slits on the skin, too.

Place the roast in a glass baking dish and cover it tightly with plastic wrap. Let sit in the refrigerator for 24 hours.

Take the roast out of the refrigerator 2 hours before you plan to cook it.

Preheat the oven to 350°F.

Put the porchetta on a V-shaped rack in a roasting pan and put it in the oven. Let it roast, undisturbed, for 3½ hours. There is no need to baste it, since the fat coming out of the meat will do the basting on its own. The roast should be done at the end of the 3½ hours, but you can check by inserting a thermometer, which should read 180°F.

Remove the porchetta from the oven and let cool for at least 2 hours before cutting and serving it either cool or at room temperature. If serving the next day, place in the refrigerator, but make sure you remove it 2 hours ahead of time and let it come to room temperature.

To cut the porchetta, use a slightly serrated knife, which will help you slice through the rind. An electric knife works quite well; a bread knife also does the trick. Cut the porchetta into ½-inch slices and lay them out on a platter to serve.

Ciambelline al Vino

WINE BISCOTTI

These dry, not overly sweet cookies are served all over Lazio. Every meal in Ariccia ends with a basket of them. The anise-flavored cookies are perfect for dipping into the slightly sweet Romanella red wine the fraschette have on tap. And if for some reason you don't like the taste of anise seed, you can leave that out. I've made them with chopped rosemary as well as flecks of chocolate, and they are always delicious. These are good eaten on their own, but even better dipped in red wine! **MAKES 24 COOKIES**

2¼ to 3¼ cups of all-purpose flour

1 teaspoon of baking powder

Pinch of sea salt

2 tablespoons of anise seed

½ cup of sugar, plus more for coating

½ cup of extra-virgin olive oil

1 cup of dry red wine

Preheat the oven to 350°F. Line a baking sheet with parchment paper. Prepare a small bowl with sugar for coating the cookies.

Put 2¼ cups flour, the baking powder, salt, and anise seed in a separate small bowl. Mix with a fork to combine well.

Put ½ cup sugar, the olive oil, and wine in a large mixing bowl. Add the flour mixture, mixing with a wooden spoon until well combined. The dough should be quite stiff and not sticky. If it seems too wet, add a bit more flour, up to 1 cup. Use your hands to finish mixing.

Break off a walnut-sized piece of dough and form a little 2-inch rope. Attach the two ends, pinching them together to form a ring. Gently place the ring in the bowl of sugar to coat well. Transfer to the baking sheet. Repeat with the rest of the dough.

Bake for about 25 minutes, just until they start to turn golden.

Let them cool before serving. If making ahead of time, cool completely then store in an airtight container. They will keep well for a week or more.

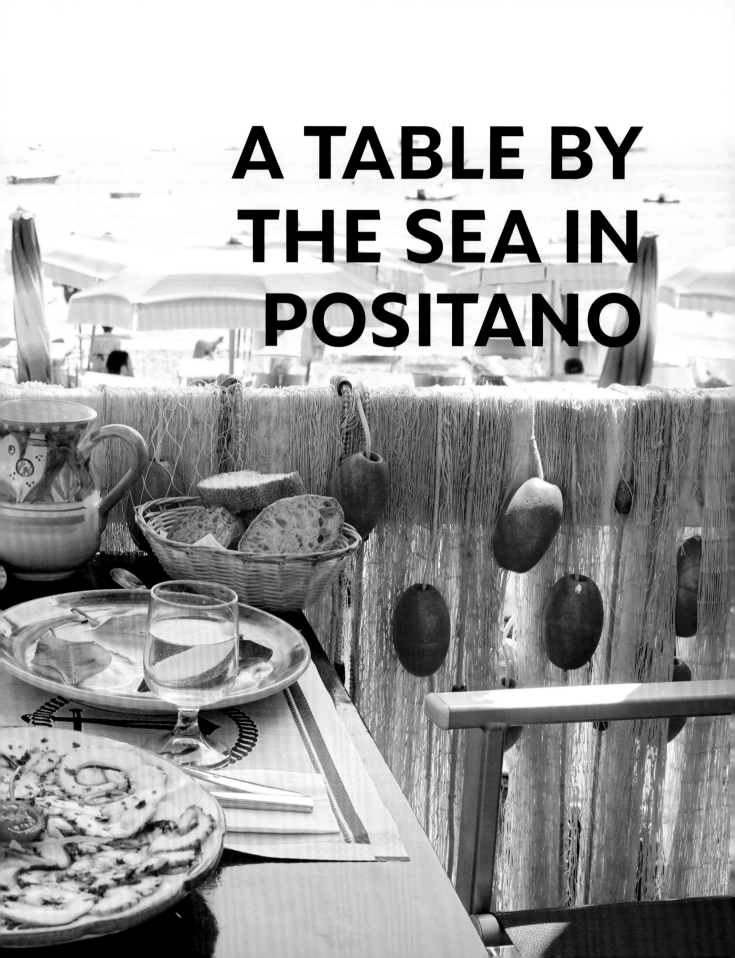

A TABLE BY THE SEA IN POSITANO

Like most activities in Italy, going to the beach is all about the food. Head to any body of water—a lake or the sea—and you'll find that the day's planning has as much to do with eating as with sunbathing and swimming. And if in the States people focus on more casual summer food like hamburgers, hot dogs, and lobster rolls sold out of shacks and eaten at sun-bleached picnic tables, in Italy it's a much more organized, and stylish, affair.

My big introduction to the world of beachy dining came in the dreamy seaside town of Positano. Located about halfway along the Amalfi coast, this tiny town full of brightly colored buildings clings to the dramatic cliffs that run down to the sparkling blue water. Although it began life as a fishing village, for the last hundred years or so it has slowly—and then more quickly—gained fame as one of the most desirable vacation spots along the Italian coast.

While the main beach, the Spiaggia Grande, is the obvious destination for getting your feet wet, with its wide sandy beach and ease of access, it's actually the smaller beaches, located in hidden coves (some of which are accessible only via boat), where the true culinary gems live.

Each beach club (*stabilimento*) rents a stretch of beach from the city of Positano. On this little scrap of unstable sand they set up not only lounge chairs and umbrellas near the water, but a temporary platform made of wood that houses a shaded restaurant, bar, and kitchen. This formula is pretty much the same not only up and down the Amalfi Coast, but almost anywhere Italians gather by the beach. The stabilimento is an Italian institution. Even if they all look similar, each one is a world unto itself and has its dedicated fans.

These beach restaurants have their own style of food that reflects not only their proximity to the sea (fish!) but also the idea that most people don't want something "heavy" when they are headed back into the water.

And so a whole menu of dishes at these restaurants shows up that a) are on the lighter side and b) don't involve a great deal of complicated cooking (remember the shack-based, temporary restaurant thing). Meat is almost nonexistent, except of course for prosciutto, which most Italians don't consider to be "real" meat. Fish is a big player, but often incorporated into a salad. In this land of sun, vegetables feature prominently because they just taste so fantastic.

My first entry into this type of meal was actually at the now-famous Da Adolfo. My friend Gillian suggested we go to what she referred to as the "hippie beach" because it was so completely disorganized and ramshackle. Three rows of lounge chairs barely fit onto the strip of rocky sand, and behind it was a shack that served some of the best food on the coast. At the time it wasn't as well known, so we had no trouble calling the night before to reserve front-row loungers and a table for lunch to enjoy simple yet authentically prepared food. The one thing we always ordered, no matter what else showed up on the barely legible chalkboard menu of the day, was a big plate full of sautéed mussels.

These days I tend to hang out at the more laid-back Fornillo Beach, sharing my love among the beach clubs Grassi, Pupetto, and Ferdinando equally. I usually divide my time between splashing in the water and lounging in the sun, with long lazy lunches followed by poking my nose in the kitchen. It is where I've eaten—and learned to cook—some of my now-favorite summer standbys: unique salads, like the one that pairs squid and walnuts, or the local specialty, caponata, which is the tomato- and tuna-filled version of the more well-known Tuscan panzanella.

The following menu features dishes from all of these places, and represents what I think is perfect beach food: fresh, delicious, but nothing that would keep you from enjoying a walk along the beach or a quick swim afterward.

One of my favorite destinations is the pocket-sized Fornillo Beach, located in the cove just up the coast from Positano. You can get there by a small boat that leaves the main pier every half hour to make the five minute ride or—as I prefer to do—meander along the kilometer-long shaded path that borders the sea, beneath bougainvillea-shaded bowers, to come out in the sparkling sun.

Like many beaches Fornillo is only set up to receive guests during the summer months. In fact, the four *stabilimenti* (beach clubs) are completely dismantled every September, only to return once the winter storms have completely passed in the very late spring. This manmade, but completely temporary, transformation of nature into something elegant, comfortable, and delicious is what makes beachside dining in Italy so ideal.

Recipe for a Party

Here are three approaches to turn this extensive menu into a party.

FAMILY STYLE: If your table is big enough, plate each dish on one or two big serving platters and place them in the center of the table so guests can help themselves. I would skip the pasta in this version of the menu.

BUFFET: If your table is too small to hold all those platters, then set up a buffet where people can help themselves. Make sure you set the table for as many people as you are serving—this isn't "eat in your lap" food. I don't think pasta is necessary for this casual option, either.

FORMAL DINNER: If you would like to hold a more traditional formal party, I recommend paring down the menu to the following: Antipasto (Sautéed Mussels or Prosciutto and Mozzarella Rolls); Primo (Jackie O's Spaghetti); Secondo (Zucchini Parmigiana); Dolce (Lemon and Prosecco Sorbet).

menu

Mozzarella al Limone
MOZZARELLA ON LEMON LEAVES 93

Involtini di Prosciutto Crudo con Fior di Latte
PROSCIUTTO AND MOZZARELLA ROLLS 95

Sauté di Cozze
SAUTÉED MUSSELS 97

Parmigiana di Zucchine
ZUCCHINI PARMIGIANA 98

Caponata Positano
POSITANO BREAD SALAD 100

Insalata di Calamari e Noce
SQUID AND WALNUT SALAD 101

Lo Spaghetto alla Jacqueline
JACKIE O'S SPAGHETTI 102

Sgroppino
LEMON AND PROSECCO SORBET 105

what to drink

WINE

White wine with peaches: I don't know the history of cutting a peach and dropping it into a pitcher of white wine, but it is a long-established tradition in Positano.

White wine: Wines to look out for are Fiano di Avellino, Greco di Tufo, and Falanghina.

WATER

A pitcher full of sparkling water, with sliced lemons floating amid the bubbles, is not only festive, but also very Amalfitano.

DIGESTIVO

Limoncello.

timing

As always, try to avoid as much last-minute preparation as possible. Here's how.

1 DAY BEFORE

Buy the mozzarella and drain in the refrigerator overnight. **Prepare the Zucchini Parmigiana. Clean the mussels** if your fishmonger hasn't done so for you. **Clean and cook the squid** and refrigerate it. **Wash and dry all of your vegetables.** Put everything except the tomatoes in the refrigerator.

Put the vodka for the sorbet in the freezer to chill.

3 HOURS BEFORE

Prepare the Prosciutto and Mozzarella Rolls up to cooking. **Take the Zucchini Parmigiana out of the refrigerator** and bring it to room temperature. I love this dish served room temperature, but you can also heat it up just before you serve it by placing it in a 350°F oven for 8 minutes. **Prepare the Positano Bread Salad** and leave it at room temperature. **Assemble the Squid and Walnut Salad.** Keep in the refrigerator until 30 minutes before serving. **Prepare the sauce for Jackie O's Spaghetti** (if serving).

WHEN YOUR GUESTS ARRIVE

Cook the Mozzarella on Lemon Leaves. Cook the Prosciutto and Mozzarella Rolls. If serving pasta, make this at the very last minute, after you have already finished your first course. **Warm up the sauce** while the pasta is cooking.

As guests arrive, **set out a pitcher of white wine with cut peaches** as your aperitivo. A bowl of olives or salted almonds is all you need for nibbles with the wine.

inspiration

SET YOUR TABLE

You can bring a bit of Positano style onto your table. The first step, if at all possible, is to head outside. If you have a garden or terrace, this is the meal to serve al fresco.

DRESSING YOUR TABLE

Most beach restaurants use paper placemats with the restaurant name on them. Available at restaurant supply companies, they are relatively inexpensive and you can even design your own in-house logo. Or just keep it simple with a blue and white border.

TABLEWARE

One of the reasons the food found in this part of the world looks so good is because it is usually served on ceramics made just down the coast in Vietri, which has about thirty producers of ceramics. By far the oldest and best known is Solimene. If you can't manage a set of Vietri dishes, stick to white tableware, but do pull out a hand-painted majolica pitcher or two if you have them.

GLASSWARE

Chunky glass tumblers for water and heavy goblets for wine are a must.

Mozzarella al Limone

MOZZARELLA ON LEMON LEAVES

This two-ingredient dish is beyond simple. Simple, that is, if you have access to a lemon tree. And fresh mozzarella. The first time I heard about this dish was from my friend Gillian, whose spiritual home is downtown Positano. She was shocked not only that I'd never tasted what she called mozzarella and lemon leaves, but that I'd never even heard about it. But the thing is, if you haven't spent time on the Amalfi coast, it's not something you'd come across in your daily life.

I tasted it for the very first time when Gillian took me to Da Adolfo restaurant. And it was love at first bite. The dish came to the table looking like a platter of leaves—which is what it was. Shiny, bright lemon leaves seared to a crisp. Peeking out from beneath was the oozing, warm star attraction: just-melted mozzarella.

Gillian dug in, showing me how it's done: using a knife, you scrape bits of the cheese off the leaves and then take a bite along with a bit of crusty bread. The hot, gooey cheese comes totally infused with the green, bright, fresh taste of the lemon trees. About as close to heaven as you can imagine.

There are two methods for making this dish. One involves blistering the leaves in a pan as the cheese melts in between, which lends it a slightly smoky flavor (pictured page 94). The other way, which the beach club restaurant at Ferdinando uses, is to gently melt the cheese, tucked in between the leaves, in a microwave (pictured opposite, bottom left). Both are good and just depend on your personal taste.

The most difficult part of this dish is getting your hands on some fresh (preferably organic, unsprayed) lemon leaves. If you live in California or Florida, that shouldn't be a problem. If you don't, ask your favorite produce store if they can get you some. An alternative is to slice a large lemon ½ inch thick, remove and discard the pulp, and then place the rings on a parchment paper–lined baking sheet. Place the mozzarella in the rings and put them in a hot oven for 2 to 3 minutes.

You'll want to start this dish a day ahead to allow the mozzarella to firm up overnight. SERVES 4

½ **pound of fresh cow's milk mozzarella**

8 **fresh organic, unsprayed lemon leaves**

Remove the mozzarella from its liquid and put it in a bowl in the refrigerator overnight so that it gets cold and firm.

{ *continues* }

When you are ready to prepare the dish, preheat the broiler to high. If your broiler is particularly hot, place an oven rack 5 inches away from the heat.

Slice the mozzarella into four pieces that are about the same size as the lemon leaves, but just a bit smaller. Lay the slices of mozzarella on top of four lemon leaves, shiny side down, and then top with the remaining four, shiny side up, making a lemon leaf sandwich.

Heat a nonstick frying pan over high heat until smoking hot.

Gently place the leaf packets on the pan, letting the leaves blister for about 90 seconds.

Gently flip them over and blister for another minute. The leaves will actually start to look burnt, turning dark-brown to black.

Using a spatula, gently transfer them to a small baking sheet and finish cooking them under the broiler for about 2 minutes to allow the cheese to finish melting. Be careful that the leaves don't burn.

Using a spatula, gently slip the packets onto a serving plate. Serve immediately, ideally with bread, while the cheese is still melted. Eat by gently scraping off the melted cheese with a knife or fork.

Involtini di Prosciutto Crudo con Fior di Latte

PROSCIUTTO AND MOZZARELLA ROLLS

This dish, served at Fornillo Beach by the beach club restaurant Ferdinando, serves that halfway hunger when you can't decide if you want a salad or something more substantial. The preparation here is for serving the involtini family style or buffet style, as either an antipasto or a main, but these can also be plated separately as an individual antipasto.

In Italy mozzarella is most often made, bought, and eaten in the same day. However, for this recipe, it's best if you use day-old mozzarella (buy it from the store that way or give the mozzarella a day to drain), so that some of the whey has more time to leach out.

An essential element in salads during the summer is the arugula that grows in this part of the world. Unlike the annual arugula, grown in hothouses all year long, this is a perennial, and its woody stems bear small, dark green leaves that are intensely peppery. They are a pain to clean, and at Ferdinando a nonna sits all day long, in her swimsuit, with a cup of espresso to keep her going, plucking off those spicy leaves. If you can't find true spicy arugula, then mixed salad greens, or regular arugula, will do. **SERVES 4 AS AN ANTIPASTO OR 2 AS A MAIN COURSE**

(pictured page 92, top right)

---

7 ounces of cow's milk mozzarella (preferably day-old)

7 ounces of thinly sliced Prosciutto di Parma (4 nice-sized slices; see Note, page 96)

4 cups of arugula or mixed salad greens, rinsed and dried

1 tablespoon of extra-virgin olive oil

1 teaspoon of white wine vinegar or freshly squeezed lemon juice

Sea salt and freshly ground black pepper

Good-quality Aceto Balsamico di Modena

If the mozzarella you bought is fresh, remove it from its liquid and put it in a bowl in the refrigerator overnight so that it gets cold and firm.

Cut the ball of mozzarella into four slices. Each slice should be about ½ inch thick and measure 2½ by 1½ inches. Place the mozzarella in a sieve over a bowl to drain for a half hour.

When ready to prepare, carefully lay out the prosciutto on a work surface. If the prosciutto slices are small, patch them together to measure about 7 by 3 inches.

{ continues }

Place a piece of mozzarella on top of each prosciutto slice, near the top. Roll up the mozzarella in the prosciutto, securing it with a toothpick if it comes apart.

Heat a nonstick frying pan to medium-high heat, and then place the prosciutto-wrapped mozzarella in the pan.

In the meantime, put the salad greens on a small platter and dress with the olive oil, white wine vinegar, and salt and pepper to taste and toss gently.

When the prosciutto starts to get crispy, about 2 minutes, gently flip the rolls over. Place a lid on the pan, and cook for another 4 to 5 minutes until the cheese starts to melt.

Remove with a spatula and place the rolls atop the greens. Drizzle with the Aceto Balsamico di Modena and serve.

NOTE When buying the prosciutto, ask if the butcher can give you four big slices from the center of the leg. If that's not possible, and your slices are too small, patch them together into the equivalent of four slices, about 7 by 3 inches, as best as you can.

Sauté di Cozze

SAUTÉED MUSSELS

This has got to be everyone's favorite seaside dish. While *vongole* (clams) are almost always served on top of pasta, mussels usually get served in their own bowl of garlicky liquid to enjoy with crusty bread. It's an extremely easy dish to make, since the mussels themselves do most of the work, opening to release their fragrant broth. Don't forget to put out crusty bread so everyone can sop up the juices. **SERVES 4**

¼ cup of extra-virgin olive oil

2 cloves of garlic, peeled

1½ cups of drained chopped tomatoes (canned or fresh), liquid reserved

4 pounds of mussels, cleaned (see Note)

Freshly ground black pepper

½ cup of chopped fresh Italian flat-leaf parsley

Pour the olive oil into a large, high-sided pan and place it over medium-high heat. Add the garlic, and when it begins to color, about 2 minutes, add the tomatoes. Let the tomatoes cook for about 5 minutes, until they have begun to break down.

Add the mussels to the pan, put the lid on, and let them cook for about 3 minutes.

Remove the lid. The mussels should all have opened. Discard any that have not. Add pepper to taste, then add the parsley, gently shaking the pan to distribute.

To serve the mussels, divide them among four deep bowls and top them with a ladleful or two of the broth from the pan. To serve them family-style, instead pile all of the mussels into a deep bowl and pour the broth over them. Either way, serve with crusty bread, and set out a bowl or two to hold the empty shells.

NOTE If possible, ask your fishmonger to clean the mussels for you by removing the beard and scrubbing off any barnacles. If you have to do it yourself, you can use steel wool to remove the barnacles. To remove the beard, carefully pull it out using a small knife and your thumb. Discard any mussels that have broken shells and rinse the rest well.

Parmigiana di Zucchine

ZUCCHINI PARMIGIANA

Everyone knows *melanzane parmigiana* with its deep-fried slices of eggplant and gooey layers of mozzarella topped with chunky tomato sauce. Based on thin slices of tender zucchini, this is the early-summer version—just a bit lighter, and certainly more attractive with its green hues. The beach club restaurant Ferdinando serves this all season long, but I particularly love it early in the summer when the zucchini are small, sweet, and tender. The other part of this dish that's essential is using the freshest basil you can find. **SERVES 4 TO 6**

2 pounds of medium zucchini, trimmed

Sea salt and freshly ground black pepper

1 cup of extra-virgin olive oil, plus more for the baking dish

12 ounces of smoked scamorza or smoked, drained mozzarella, torn or shredded

⅓ cup of fresh basil leaves

6 ounces of Parmigiano-Reggiano, grated (1½ cups)

3½ ounces of sliced prosciutto cotto (baked ham)

Cut the zucchini lengthwise into thin (¼-inch) strips. Transfer them to a colander. Salt them, using about 2 teaspoons. Let them drain for 30 minutes, until they begin to sweat. Blot them dry with paper towels.

Line a plate with paper towels. Pour the olive oil into a large frying pan, so that it comes up the sides about an inch and a half. Heat over medium-high. When the oil is hot, add zucchini slices in one uncrowded layer. (You will have to do this in several batches.) Fry the zucchini for about 4 minutes on each side, until they begin to become golden. Transfer to the paper towels to drain. Repeat with the remaining zucchini.

Preheat the oven to 350°F. Lightly oil an 8 by 10-inch ovenproof baking dish.

Place a layer of zucchini slices (one-third of the total) across the dish. Lightly season them with salt and pepper. Scatter half of the scamorza on top, half of the basil leaves, and ½ cup of the grated Parmigiano. Repeat using another third of the zucchini, all the scamorza and basil, and another ½ cup of Parmigiano. For the final layer, finish with the remaining zucchini and Parmigiano.

Bake in the oven for 12 to 15 minutes, just until the cheese starts to melt. Remove from the oven and let it sit for 5 minutes. Cut into portions and serve immediately or at room temperature.

Caponata Positano

POSITANO BREAD SALAD

You're probably thinking, What's this typical Sicilian eggplant dish—caponata—doing in the chapter on Positano? That's what I thought, too, the first time I saw it on a beachside menu. But it turns out that caponata in Positano is a completely different animal. First of all, there is no eggplant in sight. It is more like a brilliant mash-up between a caprese salad and panzanella—with some tuna thrown in.

While I've now had caponata almost everywhere in Positano, one of the best was at the restaurant Pupetto, located at the farthest end of Fornillo Beach.

You may have trouble finding rusks or twice-baked breads called *friselle* that form the basis for this dish. Made all over the south of Italy, the friselle in Positano have an extra crunch thanks to corn flour. These days, friselle are pretty widely available from Italian specialty food stores. **SERVES 4**

4 Friselle (page 222, or store-bought), or 4 slices of stale bread

4 large ripe tomatoes

5 tablespoons of extra-virgin olive oil, plus more for drizzling

1½ teaspoons of sea salt

12 ounces of fresh mozzarella, cubed (about 2 cups)

One 8-ounce jar of tuna packed in olive oil, drained

½ cup of chopped celery

½ cup of black or green olives, pitted if desired

2 small bunches of arugula, rinsed and dried

10 fresh basil leaves, torn

Soak the friselle in cold water for about 3 minutes to slightly soften them.

Remove them from the water, letting the excess water drain away. Break them up roughly and place them in a large shallow bowl. (If using stale bread, just crumble the bread into the bowl.)

Chop the tomatoes into 1-inch chunks, place them in a separate bowl, and dress them with the olive oil and salt. Stir them and let them sit for about 10 minutes, to let the juices seep out.

Using a spoon, place the tomatoes and any juices on top of the friselle. Toss them. Add the mozzarella, tuna, celery, olives, arugula, and basil and toss again. Drizzle with more olive oil and let sit another half hour to let the bread soften and absorb the rest of the tomato juices and olive oil.

Pile the salad onto a platter with a slightly raised edge. Serve at room temperature.

Insalata di Calamari e Noce

SQUID AND WALNUT SALAD

On the small beach of Fornillo, Positano, I like to visit as many of the restaurants lining the shore as possible, since they are always thinking up new and unexpected combinations of local ingredients that result in delicious and surprising dishes. A recent favorite was this squid salad with walnuts I enjoyed at Grassi. Yes, nuts and fish. Who would have thought? I'd never heard of this combination before, but I guess it makes sense. Walnuts from nearby Sorrento are world famous. And squid? That takes no justification to appear on any seaside menu. **SERVES 4 TO 6**

2 pounds of squid, inner ink sacks and quills removed (ask your fishmonger to do this)

1 large bunch of arugula, rinsed, dried, and torn into pieces, or 2 to 3 cups mixed salad greens

½ cup of roughly chopped walnuts

3 tablespoons of extra-virgin olive oil

1 to 2 tablespoons of freshly squeezed lemon juice

Sea salt and freshly ground black pepper

Prepare the squid by cutting off the tentacles and slicing them into bite-sized pieces. Cut the bodies into ½-inch rings.

Prepare a large bowl of ice water.

Steam the squid in a steamer basket over boiling water for 3 minutes. Don't overcook, or they will become tough. Immediately plunge the squid into the ice water to stop the cooking. Drain the squid and pat dry.

Cover a small platter or individual dishes with a layer of arugula. Scatter the cooked squid on top and then sprinkle with the nuts. Dress with the olive oil and lemon juice and season to taste with salt and black pepper.

NOTE If you've ever had tough and chewy squid, it's because squid requires very particular cooking. You have to choose to either cook it very briefly, about 3 minutes, or else stew it for much longer, about 30 minutes. Anywhere in between results in shoe leather. For this recipe I use the short method.

Lo Spaghetto alla Jacqueline

JACKIE O'S SPAGHETTI

The Amalfi Coast stretches for 100 miles along the southern edge of the Sorrento Peninsula, and includes the bigger towns like Positano and Amalfi, as well as small fishing villages like Cetara and Praiano. In between there are countless coves where cliffs run down to the sea to meet a small patch of rocky beach. And even though many of these coves are accessible only by boat—or a tortuous footpath—some are home to the most low-key yet extremely chic restaurants in Italy.

La Tonnarella has been catering to the yachting crowd for decades. The pale-pink building nestles beneath the towering cliff, and it's on the patio that great food happens. It's a curious mix of style, with sunbathers in their bikinis lying just a few feet from tables topped with freshly starched tablecloths. You're just as likely to see someone in the latest Gucci sundress as a guy in a barely-there Speedo.

Not surprisingly, this was a favorite spot of Jackie Kennedy's during her vacations in Capri and the Amalfi Coast. It's that kind of place, although you wouldn't guess it if you just happened upon it. Her favorite dish, or so legend has it, was the chef's special pasta made with zucchini and pancetta. And while it's not much to look at (like the restaurant itself), it is, when done right, the perfect summer pasta. **SERVES 6**

¼ cup of extra-virgin olive oil

1 medium onion, chopped

1 teaspoon of sea salt, plus more for the pasta water

½ cup of diced pancetta

1 pound of small tender zucchini, cut into ¼-inch dice

1 bunch of basil, leaves only

1 pound of spaghetti

3 ounces of Parmigiano-Reggiano, grated (¾ cup)

2 tablespoons of unsalted butter

Freshly ground black pepper

Pour the olive oil into a frying pan large enough to hold all of the drained pasta later. Add the onions, and let them soften over medium heat for about 6 minutes before adding the salt. Once the onions have softened, add the pancetta. Reduce the heat to low and cook for another 10 minutes, until the pancetta has lost its pink color. Next add the zucchini and basil to the pan and continue to cook over low to medium heat, stirring every so often. Cook until the zucchini is tender, 8 to 10 minutes.

In the meantime, bring a large pot of salted water to boil over high heat and add the spaghetti. Bring back to a boil and cook until almost al dente.

Drain the pasta, reserving 2 cups of the cooking water. Add the pasta to the zucchini, along with 1 cup of the cooking water. Increase the heat to medium-high and finish cooking the pasta while the water evaporates. This should only take 2 to 3 minutes. Add a bit more water if needed.

Remove from the heat and add the Parmigiano and butter, stirring until blended. Season with additional salt, if needed, and black pepper. Serve immediately.

Sgroppino
LEMON AND PROSECCO SORBET

Although people drink limoncello all over Italy these days, its home base is the Amalfi coast, where lemons literally grow on trees. The secret to great limoncello are these fresh-as-can be lemons and their oil-laden zest, which provides the essential taste of true sunshine. While you can certainly try your hand at making limoncello (it's not that difficult and recipes abound on the Internet) I would suggest another, more dessert-like, version of a boozy lemon drink: *sgroppino*.

As long as you can get your hands on good lemon sorbet, the rest is easy. I like this because it has less sugary sweetness than limoncello. Although most restaurants serve sgroppino in prosecco glasses, I prefer martini glasses, which make it easier to get every last drop.

Traditionally, sgroppino is served in fish restaurants, since the astringent taste is thought to cleanse the palate. But in my opinion it's good after almost any summer meal.

The following is a recipe for one person. Simply multiply for more, but you should make no more than a six-serving batch at a time, or else the sorbet will begin to melt too much. The sgroppino will be liquid enough to sip, so you shouldn't need a spoon. It also helps if the vodka is ice cold, straight from the freezer. **SERVES 1**

⅓ cup of high-quality lemon sorbet

3 ounces of prosecco

1 ounce of vodka, chilled

If your freezer is super cold and your sorbet is frozen solid, let it rest at room temperature for about 20 minutes before beginning.

Measure out the sorbet into a large stainless-steel bowl. Add a splash of the prosecco and whisk until the sorbet becomes slushy and the prosecco is mixed in. Slowly pour in the vodka while continuing to whisk. Then add in the rest of the prosecco, stirring to mix.

Pour the sgroppino into a glass and serve immediately, as it will start to separate as it rests.

FARM TO
SICILIAN TABLE

Since I first started writing about food, Anna Tasca Lanza has loomed large in my life. Way before anyone thought of traveling to foreign lands to take cooking lessons or food-based tours, Anna began teaching cooking from her estate in the middle of Sicily. This was not a cooking school in the traditional sense, aimed at chefs perfecting their skills; it was a place where Anna invited outsiders into the closed world of Sicilian landowners not only to cook and eat, but also to focus on the table and the kitchen as an entryway into another culture.

Unfortunately, I never had the chance to meet Anna personally. She was either traveling or engaged each time I visited the Regaleali estate (I was usually a guest of the wine-making branch of the family). Yet even before the advent of social media I felt I knew Anna because her cookbooks and writings had played such a large role in creating my life in Italy. Her book, *The Heart of Sicily*, was my introduction to Sicilian cooking, and also to a way of life that seemed as far removed in space and time not only from present-day America, but even from what I had come to know as Italian.

Thankfully her daughter, Fabrizia, continues the family business, running this absolutely unique and original cooking school, and she has focused it more than ever into something that is intimately tied to the land as well as the people who tend it. Long before "farm to table" was a trendy catch-all phrase, the family and the extended community of the Regaleali estate were living this reality in the rugged and dramatic landscape of central Sicily.

The menu includes some favorite dishes I've enjoyed over the years visiting Fabrizia and her family. I have a feeling they are some of her favorites as well, since they show up so often when I'm there! Some of the dishes—like the crispy fried Ghineffi (rice balls) and the juicy Braciolettine (meat rolls)—are things that Fabrizia grew up eating. Other recipes, like the Pesto di Salvia (sage pesto), are pure Fabrizia, putting her own delicious spin on a traditional dish. But the dish that sums up the two worlds of Fabrizia and her mother is the Biancomangiare. This old-fashioned custardy dessert—with its blank white, shimmering surface—allows Fabrizia to decorate it however she wants, bringing her sense of color and style directly to the plate.

Recipe for a Party

This is by no means a typical Sicilian meal. The food prepared and eaten at this wealthy estate reflects a traditional yet privileged way of life that still survives. All of the dishes feature ingredients from the family's own estate. This use of intensely local ingredients is, for them, a given, and almost taken for granted. This is a time-intensive menu with many courses. The rice balls, while delicious, are a lot of work and really only to nibble on before the meal, so you could easily eliminate these. The caponata works nicely as an alternative antipasto for seated guests instead of as a side dish.

menu

Antipasto

Ghineffi
DEEP-FRIED RICE BALLS 112

Primo

Cavatelli con Pesto di Salvia
PASTA WITH SAGE PESTO 115

Secondo

Braciolettine
STUFFED MINI MEAT ROLLS 118

Contorni

Caponata
SICILIAN CAPONATA 121

Fagiolini Ripassati
SAUTÉED GREEN BEANS WITH BREADCRUMBS 124

Dolci

Biancomangiare
BLANCMANGE 126

what to drink

WINE

When at a wine estate the wine is always local, of course. While you can, and should, seek out the excellent wines of Tasca d'Almerita, you can also consider this an excuse to explore Sicilian wines in general. Other producers to look for are Planeta, Firriato, Benanti, and Donnafugata, as well as some of the new generation of truly excellent natural wine producers like Arianna Occhipinti and COS.

Every single meal I have ever had at Regaleali has started out with something fried—and always accompanied by a bottle of their sparkling Almerita Brut or Rosé. If you are going to go to the trouble of frying, then bubbly is the way to go.

timing

These recipes come from a large estate where a full household staff is on call. That said, you can certainly prepare this meal even if your staff consists of your right hand and your left. You'll have some last-minute things to do in the kitchen, between courses, but not too much.

1 DAY BEFORE

Prepare the risotto for the Deep-Fried Rice Balls. Prepare both the pesto and the pasta for the Pasta with Sage Pesto. Prepare the Caponata. Prepare the Blancmange.

4 HOURS BEFORE

Set the table. Prepare the Stuffed Mini Meat Rolls. Form the rice into balls for the Deep-Fried Rice Balls. Cook the Sautéed Green Beans with Breadcrumbs. Take the pesto out of the refrigerator. Chill the wine.

½ HOUR BEFORE

Set up your frying station to fry the rice balls. Preheat the oven for the meat rolls. Bring a pot of water to simmer for the pasta. (Then turn it off until you're ready to cook the pasta.)

WHEN YOUR GUESTS ARRIVE

Settle them with a glass of prosecco, and then you can fry the rice balls; they really only take 5 minutes. Place the meat rolls in the oven (but remember to set a timer; you don't want them overcooked). Bring the water back to a boil, and cook and then dress the pasta. (Take the meat rolls out of the oven.) Reheat the green beans. Serve the rest of the meal.

inspiration

SET YOUR TABLE

Regaleali and Case Vecchie have a style that is unique. It is all about history, tradition, and contradiction.

DRESSING YOUR TABLE

Fabrizia brings an artist's flair to her tables. She shops the markets of Paris for fabrics that come from Africa and buys them by the meter to be turned into custom tablecloths at home. On top of this chaotic burst of pattern she layers her family's heritage—and she highlights the work of local craftsmen, as well.

TABLEWARE AND UTENSILS

Vintage Ginori plates bear coats of arms from both sides of the family, while heavy linen napkins are embroidered with the initials of her mother as well as C.V. for *Case Vecchie*. Antique silver wine coasters share table space with rustic ceramic plates from Caltagirone.

When setting your own table, embrace the spirit of layering and contradiction. Don't be afraid of color and do seek out fabrics that you wouldn't normally use as tablecloths.

Ghineffi

DEEP-FRIED RICE BALLS

I've only ever had these little fried rice balls at Regaleali. They are basically mini versions of arancini, which are a common street food throughout Sicily. The small size makes these not only much more elegant than their street-food cousin, but also easy to eat while sipping on prosecco or spumante before a meal. Although they seem fiddly, you can prepare them up to the frying bit before guests arrive. And once you start frying, they really only take a few minutes to crisp up. This recipe makes quite a few ghineffi. In case you can't finish them all, take a cue from Regaleali and put them in chicken broth the next day.

This recipe calls for making the risotto from scratch, but of course if you have leftover risotto on hand, this is a great way to use it up. You'll need about 3 cups. MAKES 40 TO 50 GHINEFFI

For the rice

4 cups of vegetable or chicken stock

3 tablespoons of extra-virgin olive oil

1 cup of Arborio rice

2 ounces of Parmigiano-Reggiano, grated (½ cup)

2 tablespoons of unsalted butter

———

2 large eggs

⅔ cup of all-purpose flour

About 2 cups of dried breadcrumbs

About 4 cups of vegetable oil, for frying

Sea salt

If you need to make rice, heat the stock to a low simmer in a small pot. Turn off the heat. Pour the olive oil into another small pot, and heat over medium. Add the raw rice and stir with a wooden spoon to toast it. Once the rice turns a bit translucent and separates (about 3 minutes), add a ladleful of stock. As the rice absorbs the broth add more, a ladleful at a time, stirring as you do. After about 15 minutes the rice should be plump and cooked through. You may not need all the stock. (You are basically making risotto.) Remove from the heat and stir in the Parmigiano, mixing well. Stir in the butter.

Spoon the rice onto a baking sheet, spreading it out to about ½ inch thick. Let it cool completely, for at least 1 hour. This also allows the rice to dry out a bit and become somewhat sticky.

(If you are using leftover risotto, start here.)

Break the eggs into a small bowl and beat. Add the flour and 1 cup of water, using a whisk to

combine. Make sure there are no lumps. Let the batter sit for 20 minutes.

Put the breadcrumbs in a medium shallow bowl.

When the risotto has completely cooled off, use your hand to form it into small balls, about ½ inch in diameter, roughly the size of a large olive (see "A neat way to coat rice balls" below). Dip them in the batter, letting the excess drip off, and then coat them in breadcrumbs. Set them aside on a tray or baking sheet.

Pour the vegetable oil into a heavy-bottomed pan so that it comes up at least 3 inches. Heat the oil over medium-high heat to about 350°F. If you don't have a deep-frying or candy thermometer, you can test the temperature of the oil by putting in one rice ball. It should immediately start to sizzle. If it sinks to the bottom and just lies there, your oil isn't hot enough. (The trick to frying food without greasy results is to get your oil hot enough.)

Line a plate with paper towels. Deep-fry all the balls in batches, so as not to crowd them, until golden. (Each batch should take about 5 minutes.) Using a slotted spoon, scoop up the balls and set them aside on the paper towels to drain, sprinkling them with a bit of salt while hot.

Serve the first batch to your guests immediately, while piping hot, and go back to finish the next. Or else have your guests join you in the kitchen, to drink and nibble while you fry.

A neat way to coat rice balls:
To make the process a little less messy, keep one hand "wet" and the other "dry." Use one hand to pick up a bit of risotto, squeezing it into a small ball. Make 4 or 5 of them, using that hand, dropping them into the batter as you go. Now—still using the same hand— pick them up, shake them off, and drop them into the bowl of breadcrumbs. Now, switching to your other "dry" hand, scatter breadcrumbs on top of the wet balls, and gently move the balls around in the bowl so they are evenly coated. Use your "dry" hand to pick them up (now dry and coated with crumbs) and place them on a tray or baking sheet.

Cavatelli con Pesto di Salvia

PASTA WITH SAGE PESTO

I clearly remember the first time I saw Fabrizia making this recipe. The entire experience was a revelation. First of all, there was the pasta itself. I'd never been one to whip up a batch of freshly made pasta, but when Fabrizia pulled out a special cavatelli maker, I decided it was one appliance I desperately needed. Cavatelli belong to the family of pasta made from grano duro flour. The dough is firm, and usually challenging to form into shapes like cavatelli, orecchiette, and strascinati. I'd seen countless southern women turn the dough into intricate little shapes with a flick of a couple of fingers. But whenever I tried, my fingers tended to make a mess of things. Then I saw Fabrizia's little hand-cranked pasta maker transform thin rolls of dough into neat and orderly—and very impressive—cavatelli. When I asked her where she got it (expecting her to cite some artisan in Palermo), her reply: Amazon.

The second eye-opening part of this recipe was the pesto. Rather than turn to the expected basil-and-pine-nut summer combination, Fabrizia went out to the fall herb garden and gathered a big bunch of sage, and substituted local almonds for the pine nuts. While this sage pesto may look like the basil kind, the taste is much different, with an almost resiny finish that works wonderfully with the almonds. Although I use Parmigiano in the recipe below, a mild pecorino meant for grating would work just as well.

This is Fabrizia's own spin on cavatelli dough, which untraditionally uses a bit of ricotta and one egg. This recipe makes enough for ten people. Even if I rarely invite that many over, I usually make the entire recipe and leave half the cavatelli out to dry on a baking sheet at room temperature, to use later. Once dry, they will keep for a few days, or else you can place them in a ziptop bag in the freezer.

This recipe calls for hard durum wheat flour, which is called *semola di grano duro rimacinata* in Italian (it can be purchased online). When pasta is made with just grano duro, it is extremely difficult to wrangle. Here, the addition of a bit of all-purpose flour, plus the egg and ricotta, make it slightly easier, but you'll still have to use your upper-body strength to knead this dough into submission. SERVES 10

{ *continues* }

1 large egg

¼ cup of fresh ricotta

4 cups of semola di grano duro rimacinata flour, plus more for flouring the dough

1 cup of all-purpose flour

Sea salt, for the cooking water

2 recipes of Sage Pesto (recipe follows)

Grated Parmigiano-Reggiano or mild pecorino, for sprinkling

Thoroughly combine the egg, ricotta, and ¾ cup of water in a small bowl.

Mix the flours in a large bowl and make a well in the center. Pour in the ricotta mixture, and using a wooden spoon, stir the flour into the wet ingredients. When the wet ingredients have been mostly absorbed, tip the contents of the bowl onto a clean work surface and begin to knead the dough. If it is very dry and just isn't coming together, sprinkle the dough with another ¼ cup of water or a bit more if you need to (see Note, opposite). It will seem like a mess at the beginning, but the longer you knead, the more it will come together. Keep kneading until it is smooth and elastic. It will probably take 12 to 15 minutes.

Let the dough rest, covered with plastic wrap, for about a half hour.

Lightly flour a clean dish towel with a bit of grano duro. When the dough is ready, pull off a bit and shape it into a rope about ½ inch in diameter. (Keep the rest of the dough under the plastic wrap so it doesn't dry out.) Run the dough through the cavatelli maker, spreading the formed cavatelli out on the floured dish towel.

If you don't have a cavatelli maker, you can use your fingers instead. Form dough ropes as above, and cut off ½-inch pieces. Using your index finger, roll the piece across a wooden cutting board, pressing down and dragging the dough across the board while pulling so that the piece kind of rolls up on itself. As you form the cavatelli, toss them in a bit of grano duro flour, and set them aside on the floured dish towel.

Bring a large pot of salted water to boil. Add the cavatelli and cook until al dente. Start checking them after 5 minutes, since they may cook fast.

While the pasta is cooking, put the pesto in a large serving bowl and thin it out with about ½ cup of the pasta cooking water.

Drain the pasta and add it to the pesto. Gently toss until the pasta is well coated. Serve with grated cheese for sprinkling.

NOTE The amount of water needed varies, since it depends on the humidity and temperature, as well as the flour; regardless, the dough will be very stiff.

Pesto di Salvia
SAGE PESTO

MAKES 1½ CUPS; ENOUGH FOR 1 POUND OF PASTA

- **2 cups of fresh sage leaves**
- **⅓ cup of blanched raw almonds**
- **2 cloves of garlic, chopped**
- **½ to ¾ cup of extra-virgin olive oil**
- **2 ounces of Parmigiano-Reggiano or mild pecorino, grated (½ cup)**
- **Sea salt**
- **⅛ teaspoon of freshly ground black pepper**

Put the sage, almonds, and garlic in a food processor. Pulse until roughly chopped. With the blade running, drizzle in the olive oil, and continue processing until smooth.

Put the pesto into a small glass bowl, and stir in the cheese, a pinch of salt, and the pepper. Taste and adjust for salt, if necessary. Cover the bowl with plastic wrap, with the plastic touching the surface of the pesto, to keep it from oxidizing and darkening. It will keep in the refrigerator for up to a week.

Braciolettine

STUFFED MINI MEAT ROLLS

Breadcrumbs are used in traditional and inventive ways in Sicilian cooking. Often used in place of grated cheese, they are also an essential ingredient in fillings and a coating for frying. This recipe, though, takes it to another level since actual pieces of bread are coated in oil and breadcrumbs.

Anna Tasca Lanza tells the story of these small meat rolls in her first book *The Heart of Sicily.* She said they were often prepared by the *monzù* (house cook), Mario. After he made them in the morning, the family could take them on a picnic or eat them cold on a Sunday night. They are also good right out of the oven, piping hot.

Although these meat rolls get threaded on bamboo skewers (I use 10-inch skewers), don't try to cook them over a fire. The oily breadcrumbs would burn up! Instead, bake them in the oven and eat them right away as the main course for a meal, or let them cool and take them on a picnic. Be careful not to overcook them, or else they will dry out.   SERVES 4 TO 6; MAKES 4 TO 6 SKEWERS

For the stuffing

1 medium onion, chopped

3 tablespoons of extra-virgin olive oil

8 ounces of provolone cheese, cut into tiny cubes (1 cup)

½ cup of chopped fresh Italian flat-leaf parsley

4 ounces of prosciutto cotto (baked ham), cut into tiny cubes (½ cup)

3 large egg yolks, beaten

1 cup of cubed bread (about 1 slice)

Sea salt and freshly ground black pepper

———

2 pounds of beef bottom round, sliced very thin

12 slices of good-quality sandwich bread

12 to 18 bay leaves

2 onions, sliced into 6 wedges each

6 tablespoons of extra-virgin olive oil

3 cups of dried breadcrumbs

———

To make the stuffing: In a 10-inch frying pan over medium-high heat, sauté the onion in the olive oil until softened and golden, about 8 minutes. Remove from the heat and let cool. Put the provolone, parsley, prosciutto, egg yolks, and cubed bread in a medium bowl, and add the onion. Mix well, and season with salt and pepper to taste.

If the meat slices seem too thick, pound them with a meat mallet until they are about ⅛ inch thick. The pieces should measure

about 3 by 3 inches; you will need 12 to 18 pieces. If they are too long, cut them in half. Place about 1 tablespoon stuffing onto one end of each piece of meat and then roll it up tightly, tucking in the ends so that no filling escapes. Set aside.

Cut the slices of sandwich bread to about 1 by 2 inches, more or less the same size as the rolled-up beef. You will need 12 to 18 pieces.

Preheat the oven to 350°F.

Thread two bamboo skewers crosswise through the ends of the meat rolls so that the sticks are parallel. Add a bay leaf, then a wedge of onion and a piece of bread to the double skewers. Repeat in this order until you have finished using all the meat. You should have 3 or 4 pieces of meat on each pair of skewers.

Pour the olive oil into a large, deep dish, and put the breadcrumbs in another. Dip an assembled skewer first into the oil, turning it so that everything is well coated. Then roll it in the breadcrumbs, coating everything completely. Place the skewer on a baking sheet. Repeat with the other skewers.

Bake for about 25 minutes, turning them halfway through. The breadcrumb coating should be golden brown and just starting to turn crispy on the edges.

Serve immediately, or let cool to room temperature.

Caponata

SICILIAN CAPONATA

Some people compare Sicilian caponata with French ratatouille, but really, the only thing they have in common is that eggplant plays a starring role. While ratatouille is a big mess of soft stewed vegetables (it's always seemed more of a stew to me than a side dish), caponata is full of chunks of caramelized fried eggplant that is bathed in a sweet-and-sour sauce. Salty things like capers and olives play off crunchy bits of celery, and just the right amount of sweetness balances out the vinegar.

Caponata will never win any beauty prizes. There's only so much you can do with a bowl full of darkened vegetables, right? Wrong. I'm not sure who at Regaleali first had the idea of mounding the caponata into a cone and then surrounding it with hard-boiled eggs (was it Anna, Fabrizia's mother? Or a family chef?). The presentation definitely reminds me of one of those Jell-O molds from the 1950s. But with one huge difference: this stuff tastes great, and actually the pairing of the intense vinegary dish with simple hard-boiled eggs not only works well in terms of taste, but can also make this dish hearty enough for a main course. Served in smaller portions it can even act as an antipasto. This dish is best if prepared at least several hours, or a day, ahead of time, to allow the flavors to blend. SERVES 6 TO 8

2 pounds of eggplant (about 3 medium eggplants)

Sea salt

3 stalks of celery, strings removed, chopped into 1-inch pieces

3 tablespoons of capers

1 medium onion, thinly sliced

3 tablespoons of extra-virgin olive oil

¼ teaspoon of red pepper flakes (optional)

1½ cups of Tomato Sauce (recipe follows)

1 cup of pitted green olives

2 tablespoons of honey

6 tablespoons of white wine vinegar

Olive oil, for frying the eggplant (this doesn't have to be your best kind)

Freshly ground black pepper

6 hard-boiled eggs, halved or quartered (optional)

⅓ cup of chopped fresh Italian flat-leaf parsley

Cut the eggplants into 1-inch cubes. Salt the cubes and let them drain in a colander over a bowl for 1 hour.

{ *continues* }

Bring a small pot of water to a boil and blanch the celery for 3 minutes. Drain, run under cool water, and pat dry.

If using capers packed in salt, place them in a small bowl and cover with water to soak for 15 minutes before rinsing and draining.

Put the onion in a large pot with the extra-virgin olive oil, red pepper flakes (if using), and ¼ teaspoon salt, and cook over medium heat until softened and just starting to turn golden. Add the tomato sauce, olives, capers, honey, and vinegar and stir to combine. Let simmer over low heat for 10 to 15 minutes, adding a bit of water if it seems too thick. Remove the pot from the heat and let cool.

Line a plate with paper towels. Pour olive oil into a large frying pan to a depth of 2 inches and heat over medium-high heat until a drop of water sizzles in the oil. Pat the eggplant pieces dry with a clean dish towel and fry them in batches until they are golden brown, turning them every so often. This should take a few minutes per side. It's important not to crowd the eggplant, so fry them in as many batches as you need to. (The more oil you use, and the hotter it is, the less oil the eggplant will absorb and the lighter the result will be.) When each batch is ready, remove the pieces with a slotted spoon to drain on the paper towels. Repeat with the rest of the eggplant.

Add the cooked eggplant and celery to the tomato sauce and mix well. Let the mixture cool down completely and taste for seasoning.

Serve the caponata piled onto a plate in a pyramid shape, with the eggs around the rim, if using. Sprinkle with the parsley.

Sugo di Pomodoro
TOMATO SAUCE

Buying premade tomato sauce is almost unheard of in Italy. This simple sauce, used as a base in the Caponata, is easy enough to pull together in 30 minutes and much more delicious than just opening a jar.

MAKES 1½ CUPS

> ¼ cup of extra-virgin olive oil
>
> 1 large onion, finely chopped
>
> 2 cloves of garlic, finely chopped
>
> 2 cups of tomato puree
>
> Sea salt and freshly ground black pepper
>
> 1 bay leaf

Pour the olive oil into a small pot and add the onion and garlic. Cook over medium until they soften, about 8 minutes. Add the tomato puree, ¼ teaspoon salt, pepper to taste, and the bay leaf and simmer for about 20 minutes. Taste and adjust the seasoning, removing the bay leaf.

Fagiolini Ripassati

SAUTÉED GREEN BEANS WITH BREADCRUMBS

When I first asked Fabrizia for the recipe for this dish, she seemed a bit surprised by my interest in something that got thrown together to round out an otherwise starch-heavy lunch around her kitchen table.

But it's the simple recipes—a side dish of green beans, in this instance—that for me are often the most revelatory. Because even though I've probably cooked many times my weight in green beans over the years, Fabrizia used small but significant techniques and ingredients that I had never thought of—and that made all the difference. And since the "recipe" was so simple, she probably never would have included it in her cookbook. I had to be standing in her kitchen, while she was actually making it, to learn.

To start off, they were pretty fantastic beans, grown in her amazing *orto* (vegetable garden). So there's that. When you start out with beans this fresh, it doesn't take much to bring them to the next level.

The first thing she did differently was to split each bean in half lengthwise. This technique is called "frenching," and it hails from a cuisine where household and kitchen staff are not a problem. But even if you don't have staff (who does?), it is completely worth the time and effort. It's a bit tricky, but after a few you'll get the hang of it. Splitting the beans in half lengthwise makes them so tender they are almost silky.

Secondly, the beans are very well cooked in salted water—not tender-crisp as green beans tend to be in the States, but cooked thoroughly. This is not the recipe where you employ the term "al dente."

But here is the important part, which Fabrizia insists on: do not heat the olive oil before adding the seasoning. Start with cold olive oil, in the pan, and add the garlic. Then, and only then, heat gently to bring out the aroma of the garlic without letting it burn or color. "Adding things to hot oil spoils both the taste of the oil as well as what you are adding," Fabrizia told me. "Starting off cold allows the flavors to come together gently, melding, which is what you want." I have since adopted this mantra for almost all of my cooking.

Finally, there's the addition of breadcrumbs, which turn up all over the place in Sicily. "See," Fabrizia said as she stirred and stirred, "the crumbs absorb the flavored oil, coat the beans, and make a kind of creamy sauce. But obviously no cream." Who knew? SERVES 6 TO 8

2 pounds of green beans, ends trimmed if needed (freshly picked won't need)

Sea salt

⅓ cup of extra-virgin olive oil

5 cloves of garlic, peeled

8 anchovy fillets

1 cup of fine dried breadcrumbs

Prepare the green beans by splitting them in half lengthwise. Place each bean on a cutting board, then use a long knife to split them in half. Or even easier, there are all sorts of tools for this. For example, if you have an old-fashioned metal vegetable peeler and you always wondered what the little square thing at the other end was for, it's for frenching beans.

Bring a large pot of salted water to boil and add the beans. Cook until very tender, at least 10 minutes to make sure they are well done. You can take one out to test (since all beans are different); it should be very wilted. Drain and set them aside.

Pour the olive oil into a frying pan large enough to hold all the beans. Add the garlic cloves. Turn the heat to medium and slowly heat the oil. Let it cook until the garlic becomes fragrant but before it begins to color, about 4 minutes. Add the anchovies, stir once or twice, and then add the beans.

Raise the heat to medium-high and stir to coat the beans and heat them through. Stir until the anchovies dissolve, then add the breadcrumbs. Continue to stir over medium-high heat, while the breadcrumbs absorb all the flavors and until they coat the beans in a rich, thick sauce, 6 to 8 minutes.

Taste and adjust the seasoning. (Remember that the anchovies will have added a lot of salt.) Serve warm or at room temperature.

Biancomangiare

BLANCMANGE

I've always had a bit of a romantic relationship with biancomangiare, before I really even knew what it was. Called *blancmange* in French, it was that white dessert that is described in one of the opening chapters in Louisa May Alcott's *Little Women*. In that book, it was given to invalids. Soft, white, and usually decorated with either leaves or blossoms, blancmange was described as having a soft texture especially easy on sore throats, and made up of appetizing and nourishing ingredients.

Of course I'd never seen a blancmange, much less tasted one, before I landed in the kitchen at Case Vecchie. One morning, before lunch, I came in and saw a wide, shallow bowl full of shimmering, and slightly quivering, white pudding, which was scattered with flecks of emerald-green pistachio nuts and fragrant jasmine flowers. "Biancomangiare," the cook shouted at me from the kitchen where she was preparing the rest of lunch. While my brain tried to translate it into English ("white eat"?) something must have clicked and my *Little Women* memory gave me the answer: finally, blancmange!

This pudding, which can be traced back to the Middle Ages, is eaten all over Sicily, and probably made its way here via Arab influence. The base is usually milk, but almond milk can also be used (my preference). Slightly sweetened, the pudding is thickened with cornstarch.

Biancomangiare is a very old-fashioned-tasting dessert. In texture it is similar to panna cotta, but since it uses milk, not heavy cream, it is much lighter. At Regaleali, Fabrizia always pours the pudding into a low, wide bowl to set, and then decorates it with whatever is at hand: edible blossoms, nuts, or flecks of dark chocolate. But elsewhere, at Caffè Sicilia in Noto for instance, the puddings are made in little individual fluted molds, which are turned out onto plates and then decorated.

Since it doesn't have much flavor besides milk or almond, the decoration can provide both texture and taste. I love chopped pistachios for the color, but also sometimes use shaved bitter chocolate or ground cinnamon. At Case Vecchie they steep the milk with jasmine flowers first, and then scatter more across the top. SERVES 6 TO 8

½ cup plus 2 tablespoons of cornstarch

4 cups of whole milk or almond milk

¾ cup of sugar (cut the sugar down to ½ cup if using almond milk, which is usually sweeter)

Chopped pistachios or almonds, ground cinnamon, and/or chocolate flakes, for garnish

Combine the cornstarch and milk in a medium pot and whisk until there are no lumps.

Whisk in the sugar. Place over low heat and whisk continuously until it comes to a boil. Boil only for 1 minute! Once it boils, it will begin to thicken pretty quickly.

Remove from the heat and pour into a flat bowl or small dessert glasses or bowls. Cover with plastic wrap, with the plastic touching the surface. Let it cool to room temperature, then refrigerate until ready to serve.

Remove the plastic and garnish with any or all of the suggested garnishes. Serve immediately.

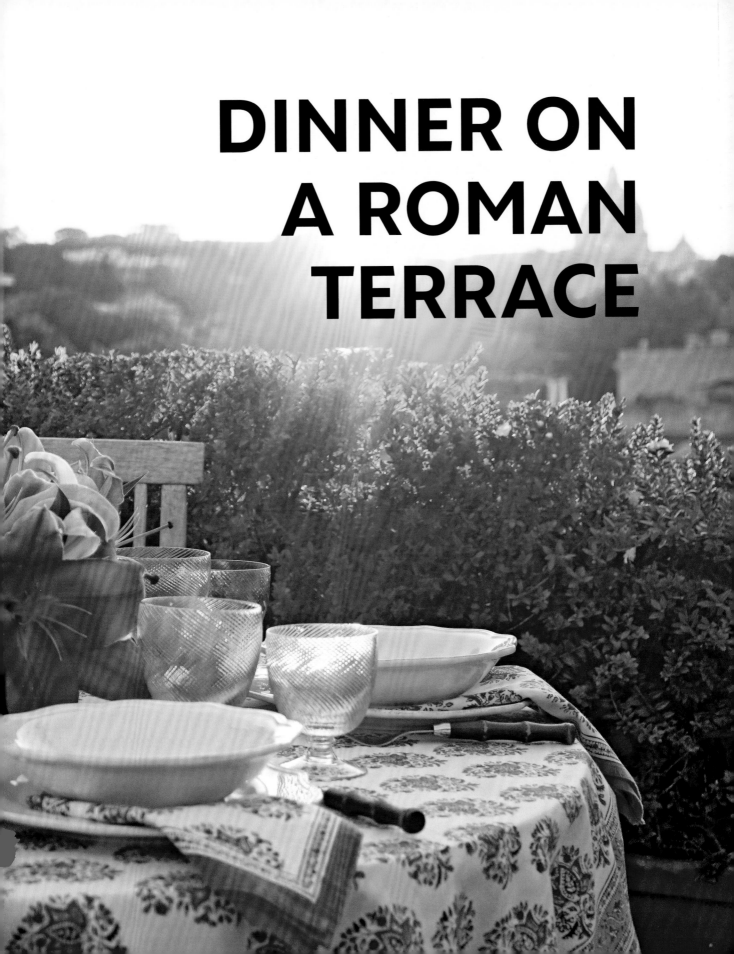

DINNER ON A ROMAN TERRACE

Most visitors to Rome—and inhabitants—dream of finding that perfect terrace with sweeping views over the rooftops and domes of this ancient city. The warm terra-cotta tiles define buildings that span the last 2,000 years and are punctuated with Baroque domes, Romanesque bell towers, and Renaissance pediments. The Tiber River glistens and tall pines and expansive parks provide the green notes in this patchwork. Gulls and swallows swoop, bells chime, and the magic light of Rome makes it an ever-changing spectacle.

Not simply content to sit back and enjoy this pageantry, most Romans would love to entertain with this magnificent backdrop. Whether that is thanks to a small balcony that can only contain a table and two chairs for morning coffee or a penthouse pergola that can host aperitivi for twenty, Romans treat their precious terraces as an extension of their homes, and the best place to gather family and friends.

It is not surprising that interior designer Alessandra Branca has fully embraced this side of Roman living. Born and raised in Rome, she has resided in the United States for the last forty years. When she decided to sink deeper roots back in Rome and buy an apartment where she and her family could spend longer amounts of time than just vacations, she had one important prerequisite: a terrace.

The terrace, like the rest of her duplex penthouse, reflects Alessandra's design philosophy of combining classic style with modern comfort. Bright colors and surprising contrasts also mirror her way of entertaining.

While Alessandra loves to cook, she is equally comfortable with handing over the reins of the kitchen to someone else while she focuses on both the setting and her guests. Yet even in her choice of help with menu planning, she mixes her Roman upbringing with her American reality.

One of the most exciting recent arrivals on the Roman cooking scene happened within the cloistered confines of the American Academy of Rome. Alice Waters took over the food program and restructured it to be completely sustainable, as well as to present local, organic, and traditional Roman ingredients in new ways that reflect her innovations in California cuisine over the last decades. Domenico Cortese was lucky enough to be one of the first chefs to collaborate with the Rome Sustainable Food Project, first working as an intern and then as the assistant chef. Today, he and his partner, Sofie Wochner, a professional pastry chef from Denmark, form one of the most exciting catering teams in Rome and one that lives, eats, and breathes this delicious juxtaposition of Italian, American, and international influences.

One of the best times to entertain on the terrace is the spring, when the days start to get longer, the evenings warmer, and when Sofie and Domenico can take advantage of seasonal treats like artichokes, fava beans, and fresh garden peas.

Recipe for a Party

This is a full and rather fancy five-course party menu, with a labor-intensive aperitivo as well as two side dishes. It is by far the most ambitious menu in this book. To lessen the workload a bit you can make the following substitutions:

Aperitivo: Instead of fried sardines, serve some ready-to-go nibbles (olives, crudités).

Primo: Buy premade ricotta-stuffed ravioli to top with the pesto.

Dolce: If making the pavlova sounds scary, buy small meringues from the bakery.

If all of this still seems like too much work and/or food, here are two alternative menus (to make with or without the substitutions).

OPTION #1

Aperitivi: olives and crudités

Primo: Pasta Cigars with Ricotta, Pecorino, and Fava Pesto

Contorno: Seared Romaine Lettuce with Fresh Goat Cheese and Herbs

Dolce: Pavlova with Crème Anglaise and Wild Strawberries

OPTION #2

Aperitivi: olives and crudités

Secondo: Confit of Guinea Hen

Contorno: Seared Romaine Lettuce with Fresh Goat Cheese and Herbs

Dolce: store-bought vanilla gelato with fresh wild strawberries on top

menu

Aperitivo

Acciughe Fritte in Tempura
ANCHOVY TEMPURA 134

Antipasto

Pesche Grigliate con Burrata e Prosciutto
SEARED PEACHES WITH BURRATA AND PROSCIUTTO 136

Primo

Sigari di Pasta Fresca con Ricotta, Pecorino e Fave
PASTA CIGARS WITH RICOTTA, PECORINO, AND FAVA PESTO 138

Secondo

Faraona Confit
CONFIT OF GUINEA HEN 142

Contorno

Lattuga Grigliata con Formaggio Fresco di Capra e Erbe Aromatiche
SEARED ROMAINE LETTUCE WITH FRESH GOAT CHEESE AND HERBS 144

Dolce

Pavlova con Crema e Fragoline
PAVLOVA WITH CRÈME ANGLAISE AND WILD STRAWBERRIES 146

what to drink

WINE

Since this is a full five-course meal, there are four different wines. You don't have to serve all four, of course, but it does add a very fun and formal element, and allows you to explore different pairings that you might otherwise not have known.

Montelvini Valdobbiadene Prosecco Superiore DOCG: This sparkler pairs perfectly with the fried anchovies. Look for any good-quality prosecco from this DOCG area.

Cantina Tollo Pecorino (a white wine): Pecorino is one of the hottest wines these days in Italy. Intensely drinkable, it pairs well with almost anything.

Franz Haas Pinot Nero (a red wine): The main course of guinea hen confit calls for a red, but nothing too heavy or full bodied.

Dessert wine: They are sweet, but not too sweet, and are a fun addition. La Cappuccina Carmenos, the *passito* (a sweet wine made from overripe, slightly dried, grapes) served at this dinner, hails from the Veneto region.

timing

2 DAYS BEFORE

Season the guinea hen (or chicken, if using) and place it in the refrigerator.

1 DAY BEFORE

Prepare the stuffing and pesto for the Pasta Cigars. **Cook the guinea hen,** let it come to room temperature, and then refrigerate. **Prepare the Tomato Oil** for the Seared Peaches with Burrata and Prosciutto. **Prepare and refrigerate the Crème Anglaise. Prepare the meringues for the pavlova;** let cool and store in an airtight container at room temperature.

2 TO 3 HOURS BEFORE

Remove all of the premade items (except the crème anglaise) from the refrigerator to come to room temperature. **Prepare the tempura batter** for the anchovies and refrigerate. **Prepare the pasta dough and stuff the pasta cigars.** Set aside until ready to boil.

WHEN YOUR GUESTS ARRIVE

Follow the directions in the recipes for the rest of the dishes, assembling the side dishes, main course, and dessert just before you serve them.

inspiration

SET YOUR TABLE

Although you may not have Rome as your backdrop, there are several ways you can bring the colors and feeling of the Roman cityscape onto your table.

DRESSING YOUR TABLE

Don't be afraid of using pattern. So often for a formal party, people pull out their best pure white cloth. Instead, use a lively print, but make sure that it is crisply ironed.

TABLEWARE

With the intense colors and patterns of the background, choose classic white plates, which do not distract from the formally plated dishes of this menu.

GLASSWARE

Any type of glassware, vintage or new, that reflects the light—Alessandra chose a Venetian pattern with a slight ripple—is always a dramatic touch.

EXTRAS

Fresh flowers from the market for the centerpiece.

Acciughe Fritte in Tempura

ANCHOVY TEMPURA

Fried food is a traditional way of beginning a Roman meal. Little nibbles like sliced zucchini, baby squid, or rice balls are often paired with something bubbly, which cuts through the richness. Domenico takes classic battered and fried fish and transforms it into something a bit lighter by making a tempura batter instead of the thicker, heavier Roman treatment. And to put his own spin on it, he adds a small dish of aioli (definitely not Italian) for dipping. The batter recipe can be used on other seasonal fried nibbles like zucchini blossoms or slices of zucchini, or even thinly sliced artichokes.

Aperitivi are a fun way to welcome guests. While Alessandra makes use of the living area of her terrace to enjoy the fried anchovies prepared by Domenico, if you are doing the frying in your kitchen, just invite your guests to join you and enjoy a glass of bubbly while nibbling on the fish hot out of the oil.   **SERVES 6**

For the tempura batter

¾ cup of all-purpose flour

1 cup of sparkling water, chilled

1 large egg yolk

For the anchovies

¾ cup of all-purpose flour

8 fresh anchovies (preferred) or fresh sardines, cleaned and bones removed

4 cups of organic sunflower seed oil or other neutral-tasting oil, for frying

Sea salt

Aioli, for dipping (optional; recipe follows)

Smoked paprika (optional)

To make the tempura batter: Put the flour in a wide, flat bowl. Slowly pour in the sparkling water, whisking it in. When it is well combined, add the egg yolk, mix well, and put the batter in the refrigerator. Leave the batter to chill for at least an hour. (For the tempura to be very crunchy, the batter must be very cold.)

To prepare the anchovies: Put the flour in a shallow dish. Pat the anchovies dry. Pour the oil into a medium pot and heat it to 350°F (a fleck of water immediately sizzles). Line a plate with paper towels.

Remove the tempura batter from the refrigerator. Dip an anchovy fillet in the flour and dredge on each side, then dip it in the tempura batter, letting the excess drain off. Gently slip the fillet into the hot oil. If the oil is hot enough, it should immediately start to sizzle. If it sinks to the bottom and just lies there, your oil isn't hot enough. As soon as it becomes golden on one side, flip onto the other. (This should only take a minute or so per side.) Once both sides are golden, using a slotted spoon, transfer it to the paper towels to drain. Sprinkle with salt. Repeat with the rest of the anchovies, one by one.

To serve, place the anchovies on a small plate with a small bowl of aioli next to them, and a sprinkle of smoked paprika around the edges of the plate, if desired.

Aioli

This garlicky mayonnaise isn't traditionally Roman at all, but makes a nice addition to the crispy fish.

MAKES ABOUT 1 CUP

1 large egg yolk, at room temperature

½ cup of extra-virgin olive oil

3 tablespoons of organic sunflower seed oil or other neutral-tasting oil

2 teaspoons of freshly squeezed lemon juice

1 clove of garlic, peeled

Sea salt and freshly ground black pepper

Put the egg yolk in a medium bowl. Using a whisk or the whisk attachment of an immersion blender, beat the yolk while very slowly adding the olive oil, then the sunflower seed oil, in a thin stream. When the mixture is well combined and thickened, add the lemon juice, garlic (grate it with a Microplane directly into the bowl), and a pinch of salt. Stir to mix it all together. Taste and adjust for seasoning with pepper and additional salt.

Pesche Grigliate con Burrata e Prosciutto

SEARED PEACHES WITH BURRATA AND PROSCIUTTO

An antipasto is meant to stimulate your appetite for the coming meal, not overwhelm it. This pairing takes a traditional rich and creamy cheese from the south of Italy, burrata, and pairs it in a decidedly un-Italian way with a grilled peach. Grilling fruit of any kind is definitely more of a California approach to things, and pairing fruit with salty foods is not very Italian, either, other than melon with prosciutto. The use of a tomato-infused olive oil dressing brings everything back to savory. (Be sure to make it the day before for optimum flavor.) The chervil is another nice, untraditional touch, but if you can't find it, basil will do nicely. **SERVES 4**

2 large ripe yellow peaches

1 tablespoon of extra-virgin olive oil

7 ounces of burrata

4 slices of Prosciutto di Parma

¼ cup of Tomato Oil (recipe follows)

1 small bunch of chervil or basil

Sea salt and freshly ground black pepper

Using a sharp knife cut each peach in half, to the pit. Gently twist the peaches to divide them in half. Remove the pits and then cut each half into three wedges.

Place a medium nonstick frying pan over high heat and add the olive oil. When it is very hot, add the peaches. Let them brown on one flesh side, then gently flip and brown on the other. You don't want them to cook, just to caramelize. As soon as they are colored, 4 to 5 minutes, transfer them to a plate to cool.

Before you assemble the antipasto, make sure all your components, including the tomato oil, are at room temperature. Cut the burrata into eight equal wedges, more or less (this is a little difficult, since the burrata is so soft).

Arrange the peaches, burrata, and prosciutto on four small plates. Dress with the tomato oil and garnish with a few chervil leaves. Season to taste with salt and pepper.

Condimento di Pomodoro
TOMATO OIL

This infused olive oil is perfect on any sort of mild cheese that usually pairs well with tomatoes, like ricotta or mozzarella. Use any leftovers on your next salad.

MAKES 1¼ CUPS

10 cherry tomatoes

Sea salt and freshly ground black pepper

6 sprigs of fresh thyme

6 large fresh basil leaves

2 cloves of garlic, peeled

1 cup of extra-virgin olive oil

Prepare a small bowl of ice water.

Bring a pot of water to a boil. Put the tomatoes in the boiling water for 5 seconds, then immediately remove them with a slotted spoon and plunge them into the ice water. When cooled, gently peel them using a knife.

Preheat the oven to 275°F.

Place the tomatoes in a small baking dish. Season them liberally with salt and pepper, then add the thyme, basil, and garlic and cover them with the olive oil. Bake for 3 hours, stirring them every so often, until soft and wilted. Remove them from the oven and let them marinate overnight, in the same dish, covered, at room temperature. If not using immediately, you can place the dressing in a closed jar and refrigerate. It will stay good for a week. When ready to use bring to room temperature, use a spoon to scoop up some of the infused oil, and drizzle it over the burrata and peaches, leaving behind the solids.

Sigari di Pasta Fresca con Ricotta, Pecorino e Fave

PASTA CIGARS WITH RICOTTA, PECORINO, AND FAVA PESTO

Ever the innovator, Domenico is always inventing new ways to frame local and seasonal ingredients with pasta. His unconventional approach often results in equal parts pasta and vegetables, or even more veggies than carbs. This somewhat California approach to primi is illustrated by his recipe for "cigars." The framework of a tube of fresh pasta is a constant, while the filling and topping change from season to season. This springtime version pairs a ricotta and zucchini blossom filling with a fresh fava bean and mint pesto. For winter nights, try the kale version, and in late summer, there is always tomato and bell pepper (recipes follow).

Since this is part of a multicourse meal, the pasta offering shouldn't be too abundant. Figure on three cigars per person. If you are using premade ricotta-stuffed ravioli in place of this recipe, serve three or four ravioli per person. SERVES 6; MAKES ABOUT 1½ CUPS PESTO

For the filling

10 ounces of fresh sheep's milk ricotta (about 1⅓ cups)

10 zucchini blossoms

5 ounces of pecorino Romano, grated (1¼ cups)

1 large egg

Sea salt and freshly ground black pepper

For the fava pesto

½ pound of shelled and cleaned fava beans (from about 3 pounds unshelled)

5 sprigs of fresh mint

1 small bunch of fresh Italian flat-leaf parsley

Grated zest and juice of ½ organic, unsprayed lemon (if using a conventional lemon, scrub it well and dry it)

¼ teaspoon of sea salt

Freshly ground black pepper

¼ cup of extra-virgin olive oil

For the pasta

1⅓ cups of all-purpose flour, plus more for rolling the dough, if needed

¾ cup of semola di grano duro rimacinata (see page 115)

2 large eggs

Sea salt

———

Grated pecorino Romano, for sprinkling

then cut the blossoms into ½-inch ribbons. Add them to the ricotta along with the grated pecorino and egg. Season with salt and pepper to taste. Mix well and put in the refrigerator until ready to use.

To make the fava pesto: Prepare a medium bowl of ice water. Bring a pot of water to a boil. Add the fava beans and boil for 30 seconds. Immediately transfer them to the ice water, using a slotted spoon.

Once the fava beans are cool, slip off and discard the outer skins. Chop the beans finely and put them in a medium bowl. Remove the mint and parsley leaves from the stems. Chop the leaves finely and add them to the fava beans. Add the lemon zest and 2 teaspoons lemon juice. Add the salt, pepper, and olive oil. Mix well to form a chunky sauce. If making a day ahead, cover with plastic wrap and place in the refrigerator.

To make the filling: Put the ricotta in a bowl. Gently wash the zucchini blossoms and pat them dry. Remove the stamen using a knife,

{ *continues* }

To make the pasta: Mix the flours and mound them up on a clean work surface. Make a well in the center and add the eggs and a pinch of salt. With a fork, break up the eggs and slowly bring in the flour from the sides, stirring it in to absorb the liquid. Once all the liquid has been absorbed into the flour, using the heel of your hand, knead the dough energetically. Knead for 10 minutes, until the dough becomes smooth, silky, and elastic. Form it into a ball, cover with plastic wrap, and let sit for a half hour.

To form the cigars: After the dough has rested for 30 minutes, cut off a fistful of it with a knife, and carefully rewrap the rest of the dough in plastic so it doesn't dry out. With your hands, press the dough into an oblong shape, and then run it through the widest setting of your pasta rolling machine. You will now have an irregular long shape. Fold both ends into the middle, over each other, into a square. Run this through the machine again, turning the dough 45 degrees so that the short side goes in first. Repeat the folding process one more time and run it through again.

If your dough is a bit sticky, you can lightly flour it. Now start running the dough through the machine, each time reducing the thickness of the setting. If you find your piece of dough is getting too long to handle, cut it in half and continue until you have run it though the narrowest setting. Lay the dough out on a clean work surface. Using a knife, cut it into equal pieces measuring 3 by 4 inches.

Fill a pastry bag, or a plastic bag with a corner cut off, with the ricotta filling. Run a line of filing along the short side of a piece of dough, leaving a border at the top, bottom, and sides. Using a pastry brush, lightly brush the border with a little water. Roll up the dough to form a cigar shape, with the filling inside. Using your fingers, pinch the ends so they stay together.

Repeat rolling, cutting, and filling the rest of the dough. As you finish the cigars, place on a lightly floured baking sheet to rest.

Bring a large pot of salted water to boil. Cook the cigars for about 45 seconds to 1 minute (any longer and they may fall apart).

To serve, place 3 cigars on each plate, and top with about 2 tablespoons of the fava bean pesto. Finish with a light sprinkle of pecorino Romano.

SEASONAL VARIATIONS:

TUSCAN KALE PESTO

This rustic and earthy pesto is perfect for winter.

MAKES ABOUT 1½ CUPS

½ cup of cooked, drained, and squeezed Tuscan (lacinato) kale (from about 1 pound kale), with 2 tablespoons kale cooking water

2 ounces of Parmigiano-Reggiano, grated (½ cup)

1 clove of garlic, peeled

¼ cup of Italian flat-leaf parsley leaves

Grated zest of ½ unsprayed lemon and juice of whole lemon (about 2 to 3 tablespoons); if using a conventional lemon, scrub it well and dry it

⅓ cup of toasted walnuts

⅓ cup of extra-virgin olive oil

Sea salt and freshly ground black pepper

Place the kale in a food processor. Add the reserved kale cooking water, Parmigiano, garlic, parsley, lemon zest, 1 tablespoon of the lemon juice, the walnuts, olive oil, ¼ teaspoon salt, and about ¼ teaspoon black pepper. Process until blended. Taste and adjust the seasoning with salt, pepper, and lemon juice.

FRESH TOMATO AND RED PEPPER PESTO

The perfect pesto that takes advantage of late-summer tomatoes and bell peppers.

SERVES 4

2 ripe sauce tomatoes (such as San Marzano)

1 clove of garlic, peeled

⅓ cup of extra-virgin olive oil

10 fresh basil leaves, cut into small pieces

¼ teaspoon of sea salt

Freshly ground black pepper

1 red bell pepper

Prepare a small bowl of ice water.

Bring a small pot of water to a boil, then add the tomatoes for only 5 to 10 seconds. Remove them and plunge them into the ice water. When cooled, peel them with a knife. Divide each tomato into four wedges. Remove and discard the seeds and cut the pulp into small cubes. Place in a clean small bowl.

Cut the garlic clove in half and add to the tomatoes along with the olive oil, basil, salt, and pepper to taste. Let marinate for 1 hour.

In the meantime, turn on a gas or electric burner to high heat. Using metal tongs, hold the pepper over the cooktop. Using the tongs, turn the pepper so that the skin blackens. Let cool.

Using a piece of paper towel, rub the blackened skin off. Using a knife, cut open the pepper, remove and discard the seeds, and cut the pulp into small cubes. Add it to the tomatoes. Let it all marinate for an additional hour.

Before using, remove the garlic.

Faraona Confit

CONFIT OF GUINEA HEN

If the words "confit" and "guinea hen" scare you off, try to have an open mind. Confit is just a fancy way of saying "baked in some kind of fat" (in this case, olive oil), and guinea hen is a delicious alternative to chicken. Sometimes called guinea fowl, in Italy *faraona* are a popular choice for farmers, since they are a bit more rustic than chickens and less prone to sickness. This means that when you do find a guinea fowl, the chances are good that it is a much healthier option than your average chicken. But the reason most cooks prefer guinea hen over chicken is because the bird has never quite been domesticated, so the flesh is darker and much more flavorful, similar to game, but retaining the tenderness of chicken. If you can't find guinea hen, then you can easily substitute six organic chicken legs or thighs. Start this recipe the night before you will serve it, as the hen or chicken needs to marinate overnight. And even though this is a meat dish, vegetables are included in two steps: for making the broth and added to the dish at the last minute. SERVES 4

One 2-pound whole guinea hen, or 6 bone-in, skin-on chicken thighs and/or legs (organic, if possible)

Sea salt and freshly ground black pepper

Strips of zest from 2 organic, unsprayed lemons (I recommend using a vegetable peeler; if using conventional lemons, scrub them well and dry them)

20 sprigs of fresh savory

10 sprigs of fresh thyme

4 cups of extra-virgin olive oil, plus more for dressing the vegetables

2 carrots, peeled

2 stalks of celery

1 white medium onion, cut in half

8 stalks of asparagus, woody stems removed

3 radishes

1 medium sweet red onion

1 cup of tender shelled fresh spring peas

1 to 3 tablespoons of freshly squeezed lemon juice

To make the confit: If you are using an entire guinea hen, separate it into parts: breasts, thighs, wings, legs, and back. Set aside the wings and back to use for the broth. If you are using chicken thighs and/or legs, set aside one piece for the broth.

Season the guinea hen legs, thighs, and breasts (or the chicken pieces) liberally with salt and pepper. Put them in a bowl, cover, and refrigerate for 24 hours.

Preheat the oven to 275°F. Let the meat come to room temperature before cooking.

Scatter the lemon zest across the bottom of 9 by 13-inch baking dish. Add the savory and thyme, and then the seasoned meat. Pour the olive oil over it all. Don't worry if a bit of the meat is sticking up, it will all cook. Bake for 4 hours, turning the pieces every so often.

Remove from the oven and let it cool for 10 minutes. Remove the meat from the pan and drain off the excess oil. Remove the skin, then remove the meat from the bones and set it aside.

To make the broth, wash the back and wings of the hen (or the reserved chicken) and place in a large pot. Cover by 1 inch with cold water and bring to a slow boil. Using a spoon, skim off the foam. Once the foam stops forming, add the carrots, celery, and white onion. Reduce the heat and simmer, partially covered, for 50 minutes.

Let it cool for 10 minutes, then set up a fine sieve over a clean pot. Strain the broth through the sieve. Discard the solids and set the broth aside.

Prepare a large bowl of ice water. Using a mandoline, thinly slice the asparagus lengthwise and the radishes into disks. Immediately plunge them into the ice bath.

Prepare a second bowl of ice water. Repeat with the red onion, slicing it into thin rings.

To assemble the dish, place a layer of peas on each of four plates, arranged in a circle about 3½ inches in diameter. (Use a metal ring to help you.) Place the deboned meat on top of this, and gently remove the ring.

Remove the vegetables from their ice water baths and spin them dry in a salad spinner. Dress them with a bit of olive oil, salt, pepper, and 1 to 3 tablespoons of lemon juice (to taste), then layer them atop the meat, creating a bit of height.

Warm the broth over low heat and put it into a pitcher.

Bring the plates to the table and pour a bit of broth around the plated food once it is in front of each guest.

Lattuga Grigliata con Formaggio Fresco di Capra e Erbe Aromatiche

SEARED ROMAINE LETTUCE WITH FRESH GOAT CHEESE AND HERBS

Why have regular salad when you can have a grilled salad? Although this salad was served as a side dish at the party, it could easily act as an antipasto, with a bit more goat cheese. In the winter, small, tender heads of Treviso radicchio make a nice alternative to a spring lettuce like romaine. **SERVES 4**

2 medium heads of romaine lettuce

Extra-virgin olive oil

Sea salt and freshly ground black pepper

1 bunch of fresh Italian flat-leaf parsley

1 bunch of fresh marjoram

1 bunch of fresh basil

1 bunch of fresh chives

7 ounces of young, crumbly goat cheese

3 tablespoons of pine nuts, toasted

Remove the tough outer leaves from the lettuce and reserve for another use. Keeping the romaine hearts intact, carefully wash them. You want to get the lettuce clean all the way down to the tender inner core. Using a sharp knife, cut each head in two, lengthwise through the core, so that the heads don't fall apart. Place them on a clean dish towel, cut side down, to drain and dry completely.

Place a large nonstick frying pan over high heat and pour in ¼ teaspoon olive oil, just enough to lightly coat the bottom. Place the lettuce halves, cut side down, in the hot pan; you may need to work in batches. Let them cook for several minutes, until the lettuce becomes nicely browned. The aim here is to brown the cut side while the rest of the lettuce remains raw. Do not overcook.

Transfer the lettuce to a plate and season with salt and pepper to taste. Let cool to room temperature.

Using a sharp knife, roughly chop the parsley, marjoram, basil, and chives.

Place the lettuce halves seared side up on a serving platter. Scatter the herbs over the lettuce, then crumble the goat cheese on top. Scatter with the pine nuts.

Season with more salt and pepper, and then drizzle liberally with extra-virgin olive oil.

Pavlova con Crema e Fragoline

PAVLOVA WITH CRÈME ANGLAISE AND WILD STRAWBERRIES

Traditionally pavlova (which is an Australian invention) is made as one large round to be divided at the table. The typical filling is whipped cream, but Sofie, a professional pastry chef, prefers to make more elegant single-serving pavlovas, and uses a richer and runny crème anglaise in addition to whipped cream. This springtime version takes advantage of wild strawberries (*fraises des bois* in French; *fragoline di bosco* in Italian) but regular strawberries cut into small pieces, or any other berries, will do nicely. If you are scared off by the idea of making the meringues, you can buy yours from a local pastry shop. **SERVES 6**

For the meringues

1¼ cups of granulated sugar

4 large egg whites, at room temperature

For assembling the pavlova

1 cup of heavy cream

Crème Anglaise (recipe follows)

4 sprigs of fresh marjoram

½ pound of wild strawberries, washed, dried, and stemmed

Confectioners' sugar, for sprinkling

Preheat the oven to 350°F.

To make the meringues: Line a baking sheet with parchment paper and spread the granulated sugar evenly over it. Place in the oven to heat for about 8 minutes.

While the sugar is heating, place the egg whites in the bowl of a stand mixer fitted with the whisk attachment. When the sugar has been cooking for almost 8 minutes, start the mixer on medium speed and let it run for a minute or so, until the whites start to froth up.

Remove the sugar from the oven and lower the temperature to 240°F.

Carefully add the sugar to the egg whites very slowly until it has all been combined. Raise the mixer speed to high and mix for 8 to 10 minutes, until the whites form stiff peaks.

To shape the individual meringues, line a cold baking sheet with parchment paper. Transfer a large dollop (about ½ cup) of the meringue to the sheet and, using two spoons, form it into a small round, about 3 inches in diameter. Repeat with the rest of the mixture, keeping the rounds about 2 inches apart. Using the back of the spoon, gently form a well in the middle of each round. Bake for about 45 minutes. At this point the meringues should be cooked through, but not too dry. Do not open the oven door during the first half hour of cooking. Remove from the oven and let cool completely.

To assemble the pavlovas: Whip the cream to soft peaks. Carefully fold in half of the crème anglaise without overworking the whipped cream too much.

Place a meringue on each serving plate. Place a nice, generous spoonful of the whipped cream–crème anglaise mixture in the well of each meringue (you may have some left over). Pour over the rest of the crème anglaise so it runs over the edges of the meringues a little. Remove the marjoram leaves from the stems and top each pavlova generously with the leaves and the strawberries. Finish with a light sprinkle of confectioners' sugar. Serve immediately.

Crème Anglaise

Crème anglaise is a great little sauce to have in your repertoire.

MAKES 2 TO 2½ CUPS

> **½ of a vanilla pod, cut lengthwise**
>
> **1 cup of heavy cream**
>
> **4 large egg yolks**
>
> **¼ cup of sugar**

Place a fine sieve over a medium heatproof bowl, and place that bowl in a shallow pan. Pour ice water into the pan, around the bowl, so that the water comes about halfway up the bowl.

Scrape the seeds out of the vanilla pod and put them in a small pot with the cream. (Don't throw out the pod: you can place it in sugar to infuse it with vanilla flavor.) Heat the cream slowly over low heat until small bubbles appear around the edge.

Whisk together the yolks and the sugar in another medium heatproof bowl until very light and pale. Add half of the warm cream in a thin stream, whisking constantly until well combined. Pour this back into the pot with the remaining cream, whisking constantly. Cook over low heat, stirring constantly with a wooden spoon, until the sauce has slightly thickened, 4 to 5 minutes.

To stop the cooking, immediately strain the sauce through the sieve into the bowl in the water bath. Stir the sauce until cool. Remove the bowl from the water bath, cover, and chill in the refrigerator until ready to use. Once you are ready to pour the sauce on top of the dessert you can transfer it to a cup with a spout or small pitcher so it is easier to pour.

LUNCH IN A RENAISSANCE GARDEN

Not everyone gets the chance to dine in a Renaissance garden. Not even in Italy, where sixteenth- and seventeenth-century gardens are lovingly preserved next to palazzi in cities and villas in the countryside. Happily, some of these jewels are attached to museums and parks and open to the public (though no eating is allowed). But others—the majority, actually— remain in private hands, behind closed gates and high walls. The owners? More often than not, the direct descendants of the patrons who commissioned and designed these living works of art centuries ago.

How does one get to pull up a chair at a private meal in one of these lush settings? Well, it helps if you are a princess, of course—which the current owners of the Castello Ruspoli, located in the town of Vignanello, north of Rome, are. Not a princess, you say? Not a problem. You can easily take your cues from one and set a similar table in your own home.

Castello Ruspoli has a bit of a double personality. The thick-walled fortress is surrounded by a moat and the location—at the edge of a cliff—was chosen not for the magnificent views, but because it was easily defended. Although the castle was home to some of the most important families in Italy, it wasn't exactly what you would call cozy. All of this changed in 1610 when a young woman named Ottavia Orsini married into the family and added some softer touches, including the immense formal garden that still stretches beyond the deep moat.

These days, a bridge spans the deep ravine, allowing easy access to what is one of the most splendid gardens in all of Italy. The design is formal, planted with geometrically laid out parterres. And although the original rosemary and sage plants have been replaced by boxwood hedges, the design otherwise remains the same.

While the long allées that bisect the garden are still perfect for the romantic strolls they were originally designed for, it is in the shaded area of the secret garden where most of the day-to-day entertaining now takes place.

Princesses Claudia and Giada Ruspoli are the current descendants of the family that oversees, maintains, and—importantly— enjoys the Castello. While the Castello is regularly open to the public, it remains the summer home of the Ruspoli family, and they use this incredible setting to entertain friends and family all through the year.

My favorite time to visit is in the early summer, when the few flowers that intrude on this verdant design are in bloom. A massive stone table sits beneath the shade of ancient trees, surrounded by hedges of pink and blue hydrangeas. The water of the fountains bubbles away in the background, while songbirds make their nests in the towering pines.

The Ruspoli family are proud of their home and take their role as custodians of history seriously. They also respect their position in the local community, and meals at the Castello often feature local dishes that draw from the culinary heritage and bounty of this area of Lazio, and come from local cooks whose families have been here for as long as the castle.

Recipe for a Party

This is a very full and formal four-course menu. If it looks like a lot of food, it is. Italians don't eat this way every day, but they often do when entertaining formally. But like all formal meals served at home, the food gets served from serving platters, not plated in the kitchen. One recommendation: after the guests have served themselves, take the platters back to the kitchen. If you'd like to pare down this menu for a simpler meal, serve either the pasta or the meat course, and skip the antipasto of crepes.

menu

Primi

Bertolacce
SAVORY CREPES 155

Fieno con Ragù
FETTUCCINE WITH MEAT RAGÙ 156

{*Pane*—Crusty Italian Bread}

Secondo

Filetto con Noccioline
PORK FILLET WITH HAZELNUTS 159

Contorni

Zucchini con Menta
ZUCCHINI WITH MINT 160

Dolce

Crucchi
CHOCOLATE AND HAZELNUT BISCOTTI 163

what to drink

WINE

This is a rather meat-heavy meal made for red wine, which is what we drank. Although Lazio is not traditionally known for its red wines, many of its wineries now make some very good reds using international varieties of grapes. Several widely available wines from Lazio that blend varietals like Merlot and Syrah into deep, dark reds with notes of red fruits, cherries, and spices pair perfectly with both the ragù and the pork. The wine we drank: Villa Tirrena, produced by Paolo and Noemia d'Amico.

timing

Princesses tend to have staff that help them take care of their castles, including cooks to make the meals. To prepare a menu this extensive, I'd suggest you follow the timing below, which gives you breathing room.

1 OR MORE DAYS BEFORE

Make the *biscotti* several days ahead of time, since they are quite hard and will keep up to a week, sealed in a ziptop bag. Make the ragù the day before and reheat before serving. It actually improves if made ahead of time. Frankly, you can even make some and freeze it to always have on hand.

3 HOURS BEFORE

Set the table. Prepare the batter for the crepes. Prepare and cook the zucchini.

2 HOURS BEFORE

Remove the ragù from the refrigerator.

1 HOUR BEFORE

Prepare and cook the pork fillet.

WHEN GUESTS ARRIVE

Invite them into the kitchen to eat the savory crepes as you make them. They are meant to be eaten piping hot.

LAST MINUTE

Reheat the ragù and cook the pasta. Reheat the pork and zucchini.

inspiration

DRESSING YOUR TABLE

The table that Princess Claudia set beneath the trees reflected the lush minimalism of the garden itself. A heavy hand-loomed, raw-linen cloth, run through with two red stripes, covered the stone table.

TABLEWARE

The dishes are adorned with the various coats of arms from the multibranched family tree. Potted citrus plants were pulled out to act as centerpieces. The bright orange color of the fruit was echoed by the thick yellow band around the pots. Family heirlooms held salt and pepper, olive oil, and vinegar, while the bread was sliced at the table atop a thick wooden cutting board.

When recreating this tablescape on your own, try to think in contrasts. This seemingly casual pairing of rough linen with crystal, silver, and family coats of arms displays the kind of casual attitude with which royalty often views itself in modern-day Italy. In other words, they don't take themselves too seriously, but at the same time show a healthy respect for tradition. It is about attaining the perfect balance between modernity and history, casual and formal.

Bertolacce

SAVORY CREPES

These savory crepes are an extremely local recipe usually made to celebrate holidays in Vignanello, the small town where Castello Ruspoli is located. Mirella, the Ruspolis' cook, originally gave me a recipe that could make over a hundred crepes, saying that she's easily made thousands at a time during local festivals. When I spent the day with her in the kitchen, I could imagine it: she had three frying pans going at once to speed things up. I've toned things down a bit to a more manageable twenty crepes that can easily serve four to six people as a nibble with drinks before dinner. They are meant to be eaten right after you make them; encourage guests to use their hands. **MAKES ABOUT 20 CREPES; SERVES 4 TO 6**

2 large eggs

2 tablespoons of extra-virgin olive oil, plus more for cooking

Pinch of sea salt

1½ cups of all-purpose flour

12 ounces of pecorino cheese, grated (3 cups)

Break the eggs into a big bowl and add the olive oil and a pinch of salt. Whisk until well combined.

Slowly add the flour to the egg mixture, whisking constantly as you add it. Add 6 cups of water, a half-cup at a time, whisking constantly to keep any lumps from forming. Let the batter, which should be quite thin, rest at room temperature for a half hour.

Brush an 8-inch nonstick frying pan with a little olive oil and heat over medium heat. When the pan is sizzling hot, using a ladle, pour in just enough batter to cover the bottom of the pan in a thin layer, swirling the pan around as you pour to distribute the batter evenly.

Let the crepe cook for about a minute. Lift up the edge and make sure it is starting to become golden. Using a spatula, flip it over to finish cooking on the other side, about 30 seconds. Don't overcook it or it will become crisp and difficult to roll up. If it is cooking too quickly, turn the heat down a bit.

Place the finished crepe on a plate, and repeat to make the rest of the crepes, adding a bit more oil as necessary. As you finish each one, lay it on top of the previous one. That way they will keep warm and moist.

To assemble, place a crepe on a clean surface and sprinkle with about 2 tablespoons of the cheese. Roll it up and place it on a serving platter. Repeat with the rest and finish by sprinkling more grated pecorino on top. Serve immediately.

Fieno con Ragù

FETTUCCINE WITH MEAT RAGÙ

Paglia e fieno, which translates as "straw and hay," is the term used in Lazio to refer to the mixture of regular fettuccine (which is a golden wheat color) with green-tinted fettuccine (which is the greenish color of fresh hay). In this part of Lazio golden fettuccine is called *fieno* even when on its own. This simple dish with a rich, meaty ragù is often served for special lunches. SERVES 6

¼ cup of extra-virgin olive oil

1 stalk of celery, finely chopped

1 carrot, finely chopped

1 medium yellow onion, finely chopped

Sea salt

7 ounces of ground beef round

7 ounces of ground pork shoulder

Three 14-ounce cans of whole San Marzano tomatoes

Freshly ground black pepper

1½ pounds of fresh fettuccine

6 ounces of Parmigiano-Reggiano, grated (1½ cups)

Pour the olive oil into a large, heavy-bottomed pot, and add the celery, carrot, onion, and 1 teaspoon salt. Turn the heat to medium-low, and cook the vegetables until softened, about 15 minutes. If the onion starts to brown, add ¼ cup water to slow it down.

Add the ground beef and pork, stirring with a wooden spoon to break them up. Cook until the meat loses its pink color, about 10 minutes.

Add the tomatoes, along with their juices. Stir well, and bring to a simmer over low heat. Cover the pot partially with a lid and let simmer for an hour, until the sauce has reduced by about one-third. Taste and adjust for seasoning with salt and pepper.

If you're making the sauce ahead of time, let it cool completely and store it in the refrigerator or freezer.

When ready to serve, heat up the sauce.

Bring a large pot of salted water to a boil. Add the pasta and cook until al dente. If using fresh pasta this should only take 5 minutes or so. If you are unsure, keep tasting the pasta. Drain the pasta and transfer it to a large shallow serving bowl. Ladle three-quarters of the sauce on the pasta and toss to coat. If you are bringing the bowl to the table, ladle the rest of the sauce on top. If you are plating the pasta individually, mix the sauce and pasta until the pasta is well coated, then put pasta in each bowl, top with a bit of the remaining sauce, and sprinkle on some Parmigiano. Serve with extra Parmigiano at the table.

Filetto con Noccioline

PORK FILLET WITH HAZELNUTS

The countryside in this part of Lazio is covered with groves of hazelnuts, which tend to appear in many dishes including this main course. The pork tenderloin is cooked first and then briefly reheated in a rich sauce of hazelnuts, milk, and stracchino cheese. Stracchino is Mirella's secret ingredient, and what gives the sauce its rich creaminess. This cheese is also called *crescenza* and usually comes packaged. If you can't find stracchino or crescenza, you can substitute mascarpone, although it will be a bit less sour. **SERVES 4 OR 5**

2 pounds of pork tenderloin (about 2 tenderloins)

2 tablespoons of chopped fresh rosemary

Sea salt and freshly ground black pepper

2 tablespoons of extra-virgin olive oil

1 cup of whole milk

3 tablespoons of stracchino (crescenza) cheese

¾ cup of toasted blanched hazelnuts, roughly chopped

Trim the tenderloins of any visible fat. Wash and pat them dry. Season the pork with the rosemary, salt, and pepper. Cover in plastic wrap and let sit at room temperature for 20 to 30 minutes.

Pour the olive oil into a heavy-bottomed pan big enough to hold the meat. Heat over medium-high heat. Add the pork. Brown it well on all sides, turning once one side is browned. (When browning meat, wait to turn it until it easily comes away from the bottom of the pan. This means it is fully browned. Try not to force it, or else bits will tear off and stick to the pan.) The browning should take about 20 minutes total.

When the meat is done browning, turn off the heat and transfer the meat to a cutting board to rest for 15 minutes.

Turn the heat back on to low and add the milk to the pan. Using a wooden spoon, scrape up the browned bits from the bottom of the pan. When it comes to a simmer and the brown bits have dissolved, add the cheese. Stir, melting the cheese, and add ½ cup of the hazelnuts. Let the sauce simmer and thicken slightly, 5 to 8 minutes. Don't worry if the cheese looks a bit curdled and separates.

Cut the tenderloin into ¾-inch-thick slices. Place the slices back into the pan with the sauce, along with any juices, and reheat. Do not overcook.

Place the meat on a serving platter. Top with the sauce and sprinkle with the remaining nuts.

Zucchine con Menta

ZUCCHINI WITH MINT

Although this recipe sounds simple, the trick is retaining the sweetness of the zucchini, which the mint enhances. At no point should either the onions or the zucchini brown. This simple dish is the perfect side to the Pork Fillet with Hazelnuts (page 159), which is also very delicate. **SERVES 4 OR 5**

1 medium white or yellow onion

¼ cup of extra-virgin olive oil

Sea salt

2 pounds of zucchini, ends trimmed

¼ cup of chopped fresh mint leaves

Chop the onion in half, and then slice very thinly.

Pour the olive oil into a large frying pan. Add the onions and ½ teaspoon salt. Turn on the heat to medium-low and cook the onions, stirring, for about 15 minutes or until softened. If the onions begin to brown, add about ¼ cup water to slow down the cooking.

Slice the zucchini down the middle, lengthwise. If the zucchini are big and appear spongy inside, then cut them again lengthwise and trim out the soft, watery inner core. Cut the zucchini into ⅓-inch-thick slices.

When the onions have softened, add the zucchini and another ½ teaspoon salt. The pan will be crowded, but that's okay. Cook the zucchini, stirring every so often, until tender, 10 to 12 minutes. Don't worry if some of the pieces are more cooked than others, but don't cook them too long or else they may turn into mush.

When the zucchini is almost done, stir in the mint, taste, and adjust the salt. Remove from the heat.

Transfer the zucchini to a serving bowl. If they have given off a lot of water, use a slotted spoon.

Crucchi

CHOCOLATE AND HAZELNUT BISCOTTI

Crucchi belong to a category of rustic cookie that shows up all over Italy with slight variations depending on local ingredients. These not only use local hazelnuts but also chocolate, which turns them a dark, intense color. Don't expect a soft, chewy cookie. These are very hard, but also very addictive. They go perfectly with coffee at the end of a meal. **MAKES 16 COOKIES**

1 cup of toasted blanched hazelnuts (preferably halved)

2 tablespoons of all-purpose flour

1 cup of unsweetened cocoa powder

1½ cups of sugar

Pinch of sea salt

2 large eggs

Preheat the oven to 325°F. Line a cookie sheet with parchment paper.

If your hazelnuts are whole, stick the point of a knife into a nut at the fat, dimpled end, and it should break in half fairly easily. Don't worry if the halves aren't perfectly even. If that seems too fussy, then just roughly chop them. Just don't chop too finely!

Put the flour, cocoa powder, sugar, and salt in a large bowl and mix to combine.

Crack the eggs into a small bowl and beat them with a fork. Add the eggs to the flour mixture and mix with a spoon. The mixture will be very dry and stiff. Use your hands to finish mixing, adding the nuts at the end.

Using your hands, form an irregular, raggedy mound of about a tablespoon of dough, and drop it onto the cookie sheet. Repeat with the rest of the dough, spacing the cookies about 1 inch apart. Bake for 20 minutes. It is hard to tell when they are done, since they are a deep, dark brown, but 20 minutes is usually good.

Remove them from the oven and let them cool completely. The cookies will be very hard on the outside and a little moist and chewy on the inside. If making them ahead, store them in an airtight container for up to a week.

EATING AT
THE MARKET
IN FLORENCE

It's always a challenge to explain the concept of a *tavola calda*. *Tavola calda* literally translates as "hot table," and refers to the steam table that keeps food warm after being prepared earlier that morning. While the closest comparison is probably an old-fashioned cafeteria, it's the kind of place where you'd be more likely to find *arista* (pork roast) and rosemary roasted potatoes than meatloaf and mashed potatoes. My first taste of a tavola calda happened in Rome, in 1972. Having just moved into an apartment located between the Tiber River and the Jewish Ghetto, my parents weren't quite ready to cook yet, but we still wanted to eat in our new home. And so we headed down the street to a tavola calda called Delfino. I can still remember the olive-green and orange early seventies interior and the bright yellow sign out front, glaring from across Largo Argentina. But what I remember most was the intense smell of roasting chickens, tomato sauce, and minestrone, which means home cooking in Italy.

While we could have eaten at one of the Formica tables, instead we did what most of our neighbors were doing: we ordered a chicken, some potatoes, and a tangle of wilted greens bathed in olive oil and garlic to go, and headed back to our new home to have one of our first meals.

The tavola calda was a pretty big deal in Italy in the sixties and seventies. It was, more or less, the first "fast-food" restaurant, in that the food was prepared ahead of time and you could eat it right away. It also offered a way to bring home precooked food, especially in cities, at a relatively low cost.

Of course the old-fashioned tavole calde have changed over the years. Many have given way to either true sit-down restaurants or else fast-food chains. But there are a few mom-and-pop-run places that still survive. One of my favorite is located in the heart of the Mercato di Sant'Ambrogio in Florence.

The Mercato di Sant'Ambrogio holds a special place in my heart for a lot of reasons, mostly because this is the market where I shopped while in Florence working on my dissertation.

It was the first real open-air Italian market that I shopped at while living on my own in Italy, cooking my way through Marcella Hazan.

And smack dab in the center of the market is Trattoria Rocco. Rocco first bought the tavola calda thirty years ago and has kept it up, making some superficial improvements and changes but essentially remaining true to its original spirit.

Rocco has never offered any kind of antipasto. "People are in a hurry, it's a workday," explained Rocco's son, Paolo. And so the menu is divided in three: primi (first courses), secondi (main courses), and dolce (desserts).

Since this is Florence, and Rocco's is basically located within a meat market, it's not surprising that most of the dishes are meat-centric. But they always offer the famous Florentine soups like Pappa al Pomodoro (tomato-bread soup) or ribollita, and in the winter, usually steaming bowls of pasta e fagioli.

Although there is nothing I love more than making the short trip up to Florence and

eating lunch at Rocco's, that isn't always possible. Fortunately, their homey, hearty food is easy enough to re-create at home and special enough to turn into a party. And since this is tavola calda fare, it means that most of the dishes can be prepared ahead of time and easily reheated. A warm primo, a meaty secondo, a crusty loaf of bread, and a straw-wrapped bottle of Chianti and it's just like I'm in Florence.

The Regulars

The clientele is still pretty much the same, too, including plenty of students, but also bank directors, lawyers, and businessmen. There are always groups of construction workers or street cleaners, and of course tourists.

Plenty of older clients obviously come here on a daily basis. They walk up to the takeaway counter, often with their dog, and even though they know the menu by heart, the daily exchange about what is fresh, what is new (there is never anything new), and how much to get is part of their routine before they head home with their tightly wrapped tin trays of food.

Recipe for a Party

To transform the menu below into a party, I would definitely plan on three courses, plus a side dish. I've divided the menu into three sections: primi, secondi, and dolce. For your menu, pick one from each section along with the contorno (side dish) of roasted peppers. If roasted peppers aren't your thing, swap in any other simply cooked vegetable like spinach, green beans, or even a mixed salad. And if you decide to switch in a rotisserie chicken for the main course, it would certainly be in keeping with the spirit of things and I for one will not judge you. For a vegetarian main course you can swap in the Zucchini Parmigiana (page 98) or Torta di Spinaci (page 43).

menu

Primi

Spaghetti alla Vigliacca
COWARD'S SPAGHETTI 170

Pappa al Pomodoro
TOMATO-BREAD SOUP 173

Secondi

Arista
PORK ROAST 174

Zucchine Ripiene
STUFFED ZUCCHINI 176

Contorno

Peperoni Arrostiti
ROASTED RED BELL PEPPERS 179

{*Pane*—Crusty Italian Bread}

Dolce

Pere Caramellate
POACHED PEARS 180

what to drink

WINE

It's always Chianti; it's local, and it pairs with every single dish on this extremely Tuscan menu. Produced in the Chianti region of Tuscany, this wine is made mostly from Sangiovese grapes. The additional label designation of Riserva means that it has been aged for at least thirty-eight months (and so more expensive, if you want to splurge). Chianti Classicos are even more prized and refined.

DIGESTIVO

Amaro. This after-dinner drink is made throughout Italy, and each version is a distinct mixture of herbs and spices, along with alcohol and sugar, that not only tastes slightly medicinal but also aids digestion.

timing

1 DAY BEFORE

Prepare and cook the following, and place in the refrigerator:

Tomato-Bread Soup:
Make this recipe up until the point where you add the bread.

Pork Roast

Stuffed Zucchini

Roasted Red Bell Peppers

Poached Pears

2 HOURS BEFORE

Remove the prepared items from the refrigerator.

WHEN YOUR GUESTS ARRIVE

Preheat the oven and begin to heat the food.

Add the bread and finish the soup.

Coward's Spaghetti: This needs to be made at the last minute, but the "sauce" can be pulled together while the pasta is cooking. If you'd like to cut the pancetta into cubes earlier, and even saute them, you will save some time on the day. Just make sure you save all the rendered fat as well.

inspiration

DRESSING YOUR TABLE

At Rocco's they use place mats made from old-fashioned, straw-colored butcher's paper. If you can find some, it also works well as long runners.

TABLEWARE AND UTENSILS

Slightly concave, heavy white plates serve to carry both first courses as well as main courses to the table. This is the heavy-duty white ceramic that is used in restaurants throughout Italy. What I really love are the small oval-shaped mini platters that are used for side dishes. The cutlery they use at Rocco's is lightweight and metal, and is the type sold at the market stands outside.

GLASSWARE

It's simple: one glass tumbler per person. Want wine? It goes in there. Want water? That too. And if you are truly an older Florentine having your lunch then you will mix both, watering down your wine so it won't interfere with your day.

EXTRAS

One of the most distinctive elements at Rocco's is of course the straw-covered bottle of Chianti (see "Wine," opposite), which is filled and refilled with the local house wine. These days any wine sold outside of Italy that is still packaged in straw is probably not a wine you are going to enjoy drinking. But I would suggest hunting down a couple of bottles. If you like the wine, then drink it. If not? Save it for cooking and then use the empty bottles to set the scene on your table, filling them with a Chianti or even using them as candlesticks.

Spaghetti alla Vigliacca

COWARD'S SPAGHETTI

This sauce is all about the pancetta. It uses a HUGE amount of pancetta per person. It is what it is. And what it is, is amazing. When my daughter Sophie and I were at Rocco's recently we got into a discussion with the owners about the amount of pancetta in the dish, because the quantity was more than you'd usually see atop a plate of pasta. Sophie was definitely on "Team More" with Rocco the chef. I felt it was a bit too much. The following recipe is the happy medium. But one thing to keep in mind is that since pancetta is the only thing going on here, try to get ahold of the best pancetta possible. Definitely do not substitute bacon and absolutely do not use anything smoked. While Trattoria Rocco makes this with run-of-the-mill spaghetti, and it's pretty great, when I make it I try to use a more artisanal brand like Faella or Gentile from Gragnano. The quality really does make a difference. You can serve the dish with ground chile pepper (Rocco sprinkles a bit along the edges of each plate). Traditionally this dish is not served with grated cheese.

If you're wondering why it's called Spaghetti alla Vigliacca, I have no idea. And after much research, seemingly no one else does either. **SERVES 4 OR 5**

¾ pound pancetta

2 tablespoons of extra-virgin olive oil, plus an additional tablespoon if needed

2 or 3 small Italian dried or fresh chile peppers (peperoncino), to taste

Sea salt, for the cooking water

1 pound of spaghetti

Minced parsley for garnish

Pancetta often comes with the skin attached; if so, trim this off with a sharp knife. Slice the pancetta against the grain into ¼-inch slices. Cut each slice into ¼-inch pieces, across the rows of fat, resulting in about 1½ cups of little log-shaped, fat-striated pieces.

Pour the olive oil into a pan large enough to fit the drained pasta later, then add the pancetta and chile peppers. Turn on the heat to medium-low and let the pancetta cook slowly and render its fat slowly. The desired texture is chewy; it shouldn't burn or even become crispy. While you are cooking it, if it looks very dry, as if there isn't enough fat, add another tablespoon of olive oil. You can tell it is done when the fat loses its translucent look and becomes opaque. It should take 10 minutes or so. Remove from the heat.

Bring a large pot of salted water to boil. Add the spaghetti and cook until almost al dente. Drain, reserving 1 cup of the pasta water. Add the pasta to the pan with the pancetta, along with the reserved pasta water. Turn up the heat and finish cooking the pasta, mixing well to distribute the pancetta and fats over the strands of spaghetti. Garnish with the parsley. Serve immediately.

NOTE The pancetta pieces tend to congregate at the bottom of the pan or bowl. When serving, stir well and make sure everyone gets their fair share of pancetta!

Pappa al Pomodoro

TOMATO-BREAD SOUP

Pappa al pomodoro is one of those *cucina povera* dishes that makes the most out of very little. Leftover bread is thrown into a pot of stewed tomatoes and *ecco!* It's one of the most delicious tomato dishes known to man—and ridiculously easy to make.

This is a quintessentially Tuscan dish, and I've actually never had it outside of some of my favorite restaurants in Florence. While I often use fresh San Marzano tomatoes, you can easily make it with good-quality canned ones as Rocco does. Either way, I usually chop the peeled tomatoes in the food processor, which makes it easier to keep all the juices.

Trust me, drizzling the dish with extra olive oil when serving is essential. Garnishing with fresh basil isn't, but it sure looks nice. **SERVES 8**

⅓ cup of extra-virgin olive oil, plus more for serving

1 large onion, finely chopped

4 cloves of garlic, finely chopped

4 pounds of fresh San Marzano tomatoes or any meaty tomato, peeled (see Note) and chopped, or two 28-ounce cans of high-quality whole peeled San Marzano tomatoes, drained and chopped

1½ teaspoons of sea salt

3 to 4 cups of vegetable broth

Six ½-inch slices of stale country bread (preferably unsalted and with a tight, uniform crumb)

½ cup of fresh basil leaves, plus more for garnish if desired

Pour the olive oil into a large soup pot and set over medium heat. Add the onions and let them soften for about 10 minutes, stirring every so often. Don't let them brown. Add the garlic and stir. Add the tomatoes and their juices and the salt and let simmer for about 25 minutes. If it gets too thick, and seems to be sticking to the bottom of the pan, then add some water.

Add the vegetable broth and stir well to combine. Add the bread. Remove from heat, add the basil, and cover. Let sit for a half hour, so that the bread falls apart and becomes mushy. Use a wooden spoon to break up the bits of bread.

Serve slightly warm or at room temperature in bowls, drizzled with olive oil and garnished with basil leaves (optional). The soup will be very thick—just about thick enough to eat with a fork.

NOTE To peel the tomatoes (if using fresh ones), bring a large pot of water to a boil. Dip the tomatoes in the boiling water for about 20 seconds. Let them cool, then peel them.

Arista

PORK ROAST

I think there may be a law that says that every restaurant in Florence must serve arista. While it may look simple, there are several keys to ensuring that yours is as good as in Italy. Make sure you thoroughly season your roast. When in doubt, add more salt. And definitely let the outside brown well in the oven. Arista is always served thinly sliced, and must be cooled off completely before slicing. **SERVES 4 OR 5**

12 small sprigs of fresh rosemary

20 fresh sage leaves

3 cloves of garlic, peeled

Sea salt

½ teaspoon of freshly ground black pepper

2 tablespoons of extra-virgin olive oil, plus more for the pan

2-pound boneless pork loin roast

1 cup of dry white wine

Preheat the oven to 400°F.

Strip the leaves off 6 of the rosemary sprigs. Place the rosemary leaves, sage, garlic, 1 teaspoon salt, and the pepper on a cutting board and chop very finely. Transfer to a small bowl and mix in the olive oil.

Rinse the pork roast under cool water, and pat dry. Place the roast on a level surface, and using a sharp knife, make small but deep cuts all over the roast, 15 to 20 cuts in all.

Using your fingers, stuff two-thirds of the herb mixture into the holes. Rub the rest of the mixture onto the outside of the meat.

To tie up your roast, place 3 rosemary sprigs on the top side of the roast and 3 on the bottom. Using kitchen twine, tie up the roast evenly widthwise, from one end to the other, making sure to catch the rosemary sprigs on either side. Salt the roast well on all sides.

Pour a bit of olive oil to coat the bottom of a low-edged pan only a little bigger than the roast, turning the roast in the pan to coat it with some of the oil. Place the pan in the oven and roast the pork for 15 minutes.

Add the white wine to the pan, and reduce the temperature to 350°F. Continue to cook for an hour and 15 minutes, basting with the white wine and turning the roast so that it browns on all sides, about every 15 minutes. By the end of the 1 hour and 15 minutes it should be done, and the internal temperature should be 140°F.

Take the roast out of the oven. Let cool completely, for at least 2 hours, before slicing.

Arista is often served at room temperature, but to reheat it, place the sliced meat in the oven, covered. Whether served at room temperature or reheated, drizzle some of the pan juices over it.

Zucchine Ripiene

STUFFED ZUCCHINI

Stuffed vegetables are a traditional tavola calda dish. That's not only because you get both a main course and a side dish together, but also because they come in their own natural portioned sizes. While many cooks choose long zucchini for this dish, using a tool like an apple corer to carefully hollow out the tubes, Rocco prefers a much more manageable small, round zucchini, called Roly Poly, which are easier to stuff and cook and look so cute. SERVES 6 AS AN ANTIPASTO, 3 AS A MAIN DISH

1 medium potato

1 thick slice of country bread, with a tight, uniform crumb

⅓ cup of whole milk

6 small, round zucchini (about 2 pounds)

3½ ounces of ground pork (about ½ cup)

3½ ounces of ground turkey breast (about ½ cup)

1 tablespoon of extra-virgin olive oil, plus more for drizzling

½ teaspoon of sea salt, plus more to taste

½ teaspoon of freshly ground black pepper

1 large egg

2 tablespoons of chopped Italian flat-leaf parsley

1 clove of garlic, peeled

2 ounces of Parmigiano-Reggiano, grated (½ cup)

½ cup of tomato puree

½ cup of vegetable broth

Preheat the oven to 350°F.

Place the potato in a small pot and add water to cover by about an inch. Boil the potato until done; it should be tender enough to insert a fork easily. Drain the potato and when it is cool enough to handle, slip the skin off. Mash the potato using either a fork or a food mill; place in a large bowl. Set aside.

Soak the bread in the milk in a small bowl.

Cut the stem end off each zucchini, about ¾-inch down from the top, and set them aside. (These will be the little "lids" that will top each of the stuffed zucchini.) To hollow out each zucchini, use a small melon baller or spoon. (The melon baller works perfectly, with less risk of breaking through the outside of the skin.) Hold a zucchini in the palm of one hand, and with the other, gently scoop out the inner flesh, leaving a ⅓-inch-thick layer. (Save the pulp for another purpose, such as a future minestrone or pasta sauce, by freezing it.) If the zucchini doesn't stand up on its own, trim a bit off the bottom to give it a flat surface so it doesn't topple over; hollow out the remaining zucchini.

To make the stuffing, add the ground pork and turkey, olive oil, salt, pepper, egg, and parsley to the potato. Add the garlic, either grating it on a Microplane or using a garlic press. Take the bread from the milk, squeeze it, and crumble it into the bowl. Using your hands, mix everything together until completely blended.

Salt the inside of each of the zucchini, using about ¼ teaspoon per zucchini, and then add about a tablespoon of grated Parmigiano, coating the inside. Using a small spoon, divide the stuffing among the zucchini, and put the lid on each one.

Place the zucchini in an ovenproof dish large enough to hold all of them. Drizzle a bit of olive oil over each, and season the tops with salt. Bake for 45 minutes.

Add the tomato purée and broth to the pan, pouring them around the zucchini, and continue baking for another 30 minutes. The zucchini are done when the tines of a fork are easily inserted.

Remove from the oven and let sit for at least 15 minutes before serving with a bit of the pan sauce. These are good warm, as well as room temperature.

Peperoni Arrostiti

ROASTED RED BELL PEPPERS

Rocco's approach to vegetables is no-nonsense: fresh produce, boiled or roasted until done and seasoned with olive oil and salt. This pretty much sums up most of his sides. I've followed his lead here using red peppers, but with one exception: lemon. While the squeeze of lemon juice and dusting of lemon zest are certainly not his style (way too fancy), they really do brighten things up. **SERVES 4 OR 5**

(pictured pages 164–165)

3 large red bell peppers

3 tablespoons of extra-virgin olive oil

Sea salt

**1 organic, unsprayed lemon
(if using a conventional lemon,
scrub it well and dry it)**

Preheat the oven to 350°F. Line a baking sheet with parchment paper.

Using a sharp knife, cut out the stem of each bell pepper. Cut the peppers in half lengthwise, and remove any seeds and the white pith.

Slice the peppers lengthwise into ½-inch strips. Place in a bowl and gently toss with the olive oil.

Lay the peppers in one layer on the baking sheet. If they are too crowded, then use two parchment-lined sheets. Season generously with salt.

Roast until very tender, about 30 minutes.

Place on a serving platter, and using a Microplane or box grater, grate the zest of the lemon directly onto the peppers. Cut the lemon in half and squeeze the juice on top. Serve warm or at room temperature.

Pere Caramellate

CARAMELIZED PEARS

What happened to having fresh fruit for dessert? When I was growing up in Italy in the 1970s, a big bowl of fresh fruit would always show up at the table after a meal in a restaurant. The other dessert option was cooked fruit. Poached pears or baked apples were the "fancy" version of the fruit course. It's getting much rarer these days for such simple sweets to show up, but Rocco's always has some form of cooked fruit, as well as a big tureen full of *macedonia* (fresh fruit salad). I am in love with his caramelized pears. Poached in wine and sugar, the pears' final dramatic touch is a drizzle of dark caramel and some totally decorative orange slices, grapes, and bay leaves. When I'm at home, I keep mine a bit simpler, but they come out just as delicious.

Almost any pear will work for this recipe. What you don't want is an overly ripe, juicy pear; they will fall apart. Look for a pear that is ripe but firm, like a Bosc or an Anjou. But really? Once you boil them in this sweet mixture, almost any pear will taste heavenly. If you like, you can substitute red wine in the poaching liquid, which will result in the pears turning a ruby color, which is also pretty. SERVES 6

6 firm, ripe medium pears

2 cups of dry white wine

2 cups of sugar

3 sticks of cinnamon

6 cloves

Wash, then peel the pears, keeping the stem (if there is one) attached.

Put the wine and sugar into a pot big enough to hold all the pears more or less upright. Heat over medium-low heat and stir until the sugar dissolves. Add the cinnamon, cloves, and the pears. Ideally the pears should be upright, but if they flop over, don't worry too much.

Bring to a low simmer and cover the pot. Let the pears cook until they feel tender when tested with a toothpick; this should take about a half hour, but will depend upon the variety and size of your pears.

Transfer the pears to a plate and raise the heat to medium to boil down the syrup. Let it reduce until thickened and syrupy, about one-quarter of the original amount. This should take about 10 minutes.

To serve, place each pear in a small bowl and drizzle some of the syrup on top.

If you would like more of a caramel flavor, let the syrup continue to boil down until it starts to turn golden-brown, about 5 minutes more.

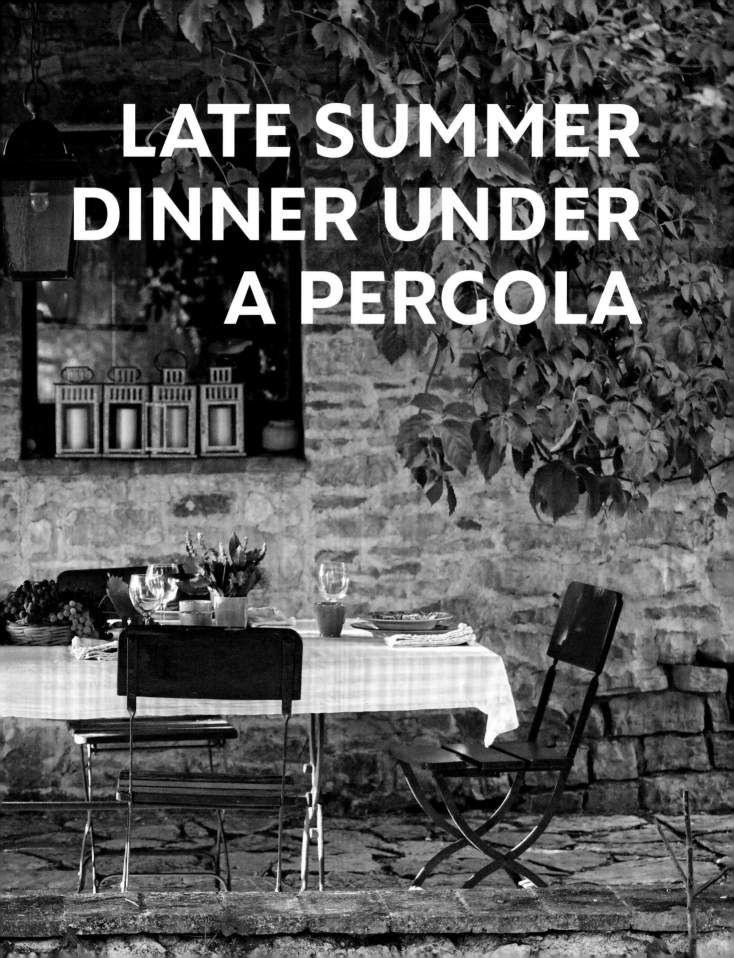

LATE SUMMER DINNER UNDER A PERGOLA

Over the last thirty years or so I have slowly but surely become Italian, adopting habits without fully realizing it. One of my favorite rituals, which I embraced from the beginning, was the great Italian exodus from cities in the summer. When the heat begins to climb in places like Milan, Florence, and Rome, mothers pack up their children and head out of town. Renting small apartments by the sea, camping out in a mother-in-law's mountain home, or heading to the family farm in the countryside are common scenarios.

I became a good Italian mamma immediately after my daughters Sophie and Emma were born. Throughout their childhood, the minute school ended, I would pack them and their Barbies up and head to the countryside. From the very beginning we chose Umbria as our destination. Since Domenico, my husband, is an architect whose work includes restoring houses in Umbria and Tuscany, this made sense. Even if he had to spend some time back in Rome at his office during the week, he could spend other days with us in whatever cottage we managed to rent.

Eventually we found our own crumbling ruin to restore, and our summer itinerary was set in stone, literally. While Sophie and Emma appreciated the chance to run around in the fresh air, I of course viewed our summer home as an opportunity to share meals with friends. Since in Rome our home was small and way too filled with children and dogs to even think of inviting people over during those years, I embraced the space and freedom that our restored farmhouse allowed.

Since most of our summer life is lived outdoors, there is so much more room to entertain. Long, lazy lunches and candlelit dinners all take place under our vine-covered pergola, where even a slight breeze and the shade mean that the summer's heat is never too much to bear.

That said, my summer menus tend toward the no-cook side of things. Sliced tomatoes and mozzarella feature prominently and when I decide to actually do some real cooking, I make Domenico light the fire outside and grill everything from bread for bruschetta to freshly picked peaches for dessert.

But a funny thing happens about mid-August. Even though it's still summer, the weather almost always turns. It's not exactly chilly, but as the days shorten, the temperatures start to drop just enough to make everyone crave something a bit more substantial than the bruschetta and grilled sausages I've been dishing up all summer.

It's also the time when our garden begins to get a bit more interesting than just zucchini and tomatoes. Fat red peppers and the first greens like Swiss chard and chicory start showing up.

While in Rome we eat mostly vegetables, in Umbria I tend to cook meat more often. During the summer, grilled meat is just so easy and good. It also has to do with sourcing what we eat. We are lucky enough to have neighbors in Umbria who are still farmers and who grow crops of sunflowers and wheat and raise sheep, chicken, pigs, and rabbits. So my menu planning usually starts with whatever meat I can get, and then proceeds from there.

LATE SUMMER DINNER UNDER A PERGOLA 185

I always make some sort of soup, from local legumes like beans or lentils, and the vegetable portion comes straight from my own garden. As the days grow shorter and the air turns cooler, I take advantage of our last weeks under the pergola, abandoning my grill to slowly braise either a chicken or a rabbit from my neighbor.

As the sun goes down, I light candles and the air grows blissfully cool. While it's not quite time to pull out sweaters and shawls, I know the days will get shorter and the temperatures will keep dropping, which makes these last nights out under the pergola so precious.

Recipe for a Party

This is a full three-course dinner, but my goal is to make it easy as well as to extend the fun. Having separate courses (plus predinner drinks, of course) stretches out the evening. That said, if you want a simpler menu, then eliminate the soup course. Alternatively, if you want to go vegetarian, then double the recipe for the stuffed bell peppers and eliminate the chicken. When I entertain I do like to set a formal table. But to make things easier, I serve the food family style and let people help themselves.

menu

Aperitivo

Salvia Fritto

FRIED SAGE LEAVES 189

Primo

Zuppa di Fagioli

GARLICKY BEAN SOUP 190

Secondo

Pollo Cacciatore

HUNTER'S CHICKEN 193

Contorni

Peperone Gratinate

STUFFED BELL PEPPERS 195

Verdura Ripassata

SAUTÉED GREENS 196

{*Pane*—Crusty Italian Bread}

Dolce

Crostata

JAM TART 197

what to drink

WINE

In this 'tween season it makes sense to choose a 'tween wine: rosé. A sparkling rosé from Puglia goes perfectly with the fried sage leaves, and also pairs well with the soup. Moving on to red with the main course is natural, especially since Umbria is known for its robust reds. Sagrantino, the most famous of them, can be a bit overwhelming, so I tend toward a Montefalco Rosso, which is mostly Sangiovese, with about 10 to 15 percent Sagrantino, along with another grape like Merlot or Cabernet Sauvignon. It's an extremely drinkable red, not too expensive, and goes well with stewed meats. Some of the producers to look out for are Caprai, Adanti, and Antonelli.

timing

The beauty of this menu is that almost everything can be made ahead of time. In fact some things, like the soup and the chicken, taste even better the following day. The only thing that needs last-minute fiddling is the fried sage leaves. But really, it's just 5 minutes of fiddling.

2 DAYS BEFORE

Soak the beans for the Garlicky Bean Soup.

1 DAY BEFORE

Make the Garlicky Bean Soup and refrigerate it. Make the Hunter's Chicken and refrigerate it. Make the Sautéed Greens and the Stuffed Bell Peppers and refrigerate them. Prepare the dough for the crostata and place it in the refrigerator.

THE MORNING OF THE MEAL

Take the crostata dough out of the refrigerator and prepare and bake the crostata. Chill the wine.

4 HOURS BEFORE

Set the table.

2 HOURS BEFORE

Take everything out of the refrigerator to come to room temperature. Prepare the batter for the Fried Sage Leaves, and pour the oil in the pan for frying.

WHEN YOUR GUESTS ARRIVE

Serve your guests drinks while you quickly fry up the sage leaves. Heat up the soup right before serving. Heat up the rest of the dishes right before serving.

NOTE: Deruta is a small town in Umbria that has been making brightly colored majolica for centuries. Ever since I wrote my first book on ceramics from this small town, I've been collecting them. There are many centers of majolica ware throughout Italy (Vietri, Caltigirone, Faenza), and many producers make lively patterns that allow you to mix and match, bringing a bit of Italy onto your table as part of a tradition that stretches back centuries.

inspiration

SET YOUR TABLE

Although I like to set a somewhat formal table (several glasses, two plates, etc., at each setting) the elements themselves are laid-back and colorful. The star of any table I set in Umbria are ceramics from nearby Deruta (see Note). For a late-summer dinner I love my set that features fruits. While I insist on using glass for wine, with water I'm much more lenient and use ceramic water cups from Sicily. The various glazes of the cups allow another layer of color and texture.

DRESSING YOUR TABLE

Like everyone else, I love the simple checked tablecloths that often show up in Italian trattorias. Since they can be hard to find, I go to fabric stores that specialize in supplying restaurants and just buy the relatively cheap material by the yard, then get tablecloths and napkins made up by a seamstress at much less cost than a fancy set.

EXTRAS

I love edible centerpieces. At this time of year, I always pull off bunches of grapes from our vines, which look great and serve as dessert. Tiny vases are full of herbs from the garden, too—rosemary and bay—with a few blossoms stolen from the pot full of geraniums by our door.

Salvia Fritto

FRIED SAGE LEAVES

If you've never had fried sage leaves, you're in for a treat. They're beyond easy, and have got to have the highest delicious-to-pretty ratio of anything I know. The dark green leaves get dipped quickly in a very simple flour-and-water batter. A few minutes in a few inches of hot olive oil, and they become crunchy, earthy treats. Sage chips, more or less.

It's something I do all summer long, and often make do with my normal-sized sage leaves. But if you are able to get your hands on the larger leaves it's much less fussy. **SERVES 6**

1 cup of water

⅓ to ½ cup of all-purpose flour

Extra-virgin olive oil

24 to 30 sage leaves

Sea salt

Place the water in a shallow bowl. Slowly add the flour, a bit at a time, stirring with a fork. Keep adding until you have a loose batter about the consistency of crepe batter. Let rest at room temperature for 15 minutes.

Heat about 1 inch of olive oil in a medium frying pan. When the oil is hot (a fleck of water will sizzle) dip the leaves in the batter and carefully place them in the pan. Work in batches so you don't crowd the pan. Use tongs to turn them after 2 to 3 minutes. When golden, transfer them to paper towels to drain. Immediately sprinkle with salt and serve.

Zuppa di Fagioli

GARLICKY BEAN SOUP

One of the things that I never think of during the heat of summer is soup. But by mid-August, when the weather cools a bit and the days start to shorten, I bring out versions of this bean soup just about every time we have friends over. A simple bean soup makes people so happy! This time of year, luckily, is when the first fresh shelling beans start to turn up, and so I use those if I can get them. But even when I can only get dried beans, this is my soup of preference.

Since it's so simple—basically beans and not much else—the quality of the beans does matter. Although you can certainly use canned beans if you must, it really won't be the same soup. One thing that makes this soup so delicious is the use of the water the beans are cooked in. Seasoned with carrot, celery, onion, and bay leaf, and full of the starch from the beans, it adds a base to the soup that you just can't get from a can.

Although the soup itself doesn't have a lot of olive oil in it, a swirl of your best extra-virgin variety is absolutely essential to finish the soup, along with a sprinkle of freshly chopped parsley. If you want to make the dish even more filling, put a piece of toasted rustic bread at the bottom of the bowl. And if you want to add more garlic, rub the toast with a clove before ladling over the soup. SERVES 5 OR 6

½ **cup of extra-virgin olive oil**

8 cloves of garlic, chopped, plus 1 clove for rubbing the bread (optional)

4 cups of cooked dried White Beans (recipe follows), with 3 cups cooking water from the beans

Sea salt and freshly ground black pepper

Rustic Italian-style bread (optional)

½ **cup of chopped fresh Italian flat-leaf parsley**

Extra-virgin olive oil, for drizzling (preferably your best variety)

Pour the olive oil into a large pot and add the garlic. Heat gently for a few minutes over low heat until the garlic begins to soften, but do not let it brown. Add the beans and give them a good stir. Add some black pepper and the reserved bean broth and bring to a simmer over low heat. Cook for about 20 minutes, covered. Since the beans are already cooked at this point, the low simmer serves to help meld the flavors.

Remove from the heat. Using an immersion blender, blend the soup just a little. (I like to have some whole beans floating around, but I also like enough pureed beans to give the watery

broth some thickness.) Taste and adjust for salt and pepper.

If you are using bread at the bottom of the bowls (and I highly recommend this!) then toast five or six ½-inch-thick slices of the bread, rub them with a peeled clove of garlic, and place them in each bowl before proceeding.

To serve, ladle the hot soup into bowls, sprinkle them with parsley, and drizzle some olive oil on top.

White Beans

CANNELLINI OR BORLOTTI

This basic recipe for cooked beans will serve not only for this soup recipe, but for any dish that uses beans. If you end up with too many cooked beans, they can be drained, stored in ziptop bags, and placed in the freezer: a much better alternative to using canned beans.

MAKES 7 CUPS COOKED BEANS

- **1 pound of dried cannellini or borlotti beans (about 2 cups)**
- **1 carrot**
- **1 stalk of celery**
- **1 medium white or yellow onion, halved**
- **1 or 2 bay leaves**
- **½ teaspoon of sea salt**

The night before you are going to make the soup, put the beans in a large bowl to soak, covered with water.

The next morning, drain and rinse the beans and put them in a large, heavy-bottomed pot.

Add water so it comes up 3 inches over the top of the beans.

Bring to a slow simmer over very low heat. As foam begins to form on the surface of the water, skim it off with a spoon and discard. Once the foam has stopped forming, add the carrot, celery, onion, bay leaves, and salt. Return to a simmer over the lowest heat possible and place the lid on, slightly askew. Cook the beans until quite tender, but be careful not to overcook them. The timing for beans varies and depends on both the size and the age of the beans. In general, most beans should be tender in 45 to 60 minutes. But testing as you go is always the best way to tell.

Remove from the heat and drain, reserving all of the cooking water. Discard the carrot, celery, onion, and bay leaf.

You will need 4 cups of beans for the Garlicky Bean Soup (page 190). Pour the excess cooled beans into a ziptop bag and freeze them, or refrigerate them and use them during the week for other dishes. They will last 4 or 5 days in the refrigerator.

Pollo Cacciatore

HUNTER'S CHICKEN

After a summer spent eating meat cooked over the grill, I'm more than ready for a dish that doesn't involve fire. This chicken dish has become a tradition at our house to usher in the change in season. *Cacciatore* translates as "hunter." The ingredients change wildly across different parts of Italy, as does the type of meat featured. Since it is the hunter's dish, it usually involves some sort of semiwild animal like rabbit, pigeon, or boar. But over the years, of course, chicken has gotten into the game as well.

While in the south of Italy you'll see either tomatoes or peppers working their way into these rustic stews, in Umbria it's a different story. The meat is usually cooked in an intense mixture of onions and herbs, with the addition of salty elements like capers and anchovies. White wine often brings it all together. I like making this version with a chicken bought from my next-door neighbor, Marisa, but if your neighbor doesn't raise chickens, try to find one as local and as organic as possible. The addition of mushrooms and a bit of prosciutto instead of the anchovies or capers give it an earthy flavor.

Will this be the same dish if you use skinless, boneless chicken breast? My answer: No. The success of this dish relies on getting the very best chicken you can, and using every last bit. The browning of the skin is what gives the sauce its flavor, and chicken cooked on the bone is much more tasty. SERVES 4 OR 5

1 large chicken (4 to 5 pounds), patted dry

2 teaspoons of sea salt

1 teaspoon of freshly ground black pepper

¼ cup of extra-virgin olive oil

2 leeks, thoroughly cleaned and thinly sliced

10 fresh sage leaves

4 sprigs of fresh rosemary

1 pound of mushrooms, cleaned and quartered

2 cloves of garlic, chopped

3½ ounces of thinly sliced prosciutto

1 cup of tomato puree

2 cups of dry white wine

¼ cup of chopped fresh Italian flat-leaf parsley

Cut the chicken into serving-sized pieces if your butcher hasn't done it already: breasts, thighs, wings, legs, and back. If the breasts are really big, chop them in two with a cleaver. Season with the salt and pepper at least 20 minutes before cooking.

{ *continues* }

Pour the olive oil into a deep frying pan large enough to hold all of the chicken without crowding. Heat over medium-high until hot. Add the chicken pieces in one layer, skin side down. Let the chicken cook until well browned, about 10 minutes. Don't flip the pieces until they are no longer sticking to the pan; this is when you know they have completely browned.

Lift the chicken out of the pan and transfer to a plate, leaving the oil and any fat behind. Reduce the heat to medium and add the leeks, sage, and rosemary. Let them cook until the leeks have wilted, about 10 minutes. As the leeks wilt they will release their liquid, which you can use to deglaze the pan with a wooden spoon. Raise the heat to medium-high and add the mushrooms. Stir them around until they start to reduce in size, about 8 minutes. Add the garlic and prosciutto and cook for a few minutes before stirring in the tomato puree. Let cook another 5 minutes, stirring every so often.

Return the chicken to the pan and stir to coat it with the sauce. Pour in the wine and let it bubble until almost evaporated, 1 to 2 minutes. Partially cover the pan with the lid and continue cooking, with the lid askew, for another 20 to 25 minutes, depending on the size of your chicken pieces. If it seems too dry, you can add ¼ cup of water. Taste and adjust for salt and pepper. The dish, as it is served in Umbria, is quite salty, also due to the addition of prosciutto.

Add the parsley right before serving, stirring it into the sauce.

Peperone Gratinate

STUFFED BELL PEPPERS

The end of summer means the end of tomatoes. Luckily, bell peppers step up to take their place. I love peppers simply roasted in the oven, but sprinkling them with highly seasoned, oily breadcrumbs makes them even better. SERVES 6

2 tablespoons of capers

1 pound of red or yellow bell peppers

Sea salt

1 cup of coarse breadcrumbs (preferably homemade)

⅓ cup of pitted black Italian olives

1 cup of fresh Italian flat-leaf parsley

½ cup of fresh basil leaves

3 anchovy fillets

2 cloves of garlic, chopped

¼ cup of extra-virgin olive oil, plus more for drizzling

Red pepper flakes

Preheat the oven to 350°F. Line a baking sheet with parchment paper.

If using capers packed in salt, place them in a small bowl and cover with water to soak for 15 minutes before rinsing and draining.

Slice the peppers in half lengthwise and carefully trim out the core and any seeds, leaving the stem. Place the peppers in one layer on the parchment, cut side up. Lightly salt them.

Place the breadcrumbs in a food processor and add the capers, olives, parsley, basil, anchovies, garlic, and olive oil. Pulse, on and off, to combine well. Taste and add salt and red pepper flakes to taste.

Divide the breadcrumb mixture among the peppers, putting about ¼ cup of the filling in each pepper (or more if the peppers are on the larger size). Drizzle with olive oil and place them in the oven for 20 to 30 minutes, until the peppers are well cooked and the stuffing starts to brown.

Remove from the oven and let cool completely.

Verdura Ripassata

SAUTÉED GREENS

When you go out to a restaurant in Umbria and ask what side dishes they have, the waiter will almost always reply, "Insalata, patate e verdura." While *verdura* translates into English as "vegetable," in this case it always refers to boiled greens. It can be spinach, Swiss chard, or most commonly, chicory—but it is always called, generically, verdura. If you ask the waiter which one it is, he will most likely just shrug his shoulders as if to say, "Why would it matter?," or sometimes he might reply, "All of them, mixed."

While I love spinach and Swiss chard, I have a soft spot for bitter greens like chicory. The trick is taming them first. To bring out the best in chicory, you have to boil it well, in abundant salted water. None of that "wilting" that goes on with other greens; here the goal is to leach out the most forward of the bitterness. Afterward, add heaps of olive oil and as much garlic and red pepper as you like. **SERVES 4 OR 5**

1 tablespoon of sea salt

3 pounds of chicory greens (if you can't find chicory greens, dandelion greens, broccoli rabe, or the sweeter spinach or Swiss chard will work, too)

¼ cup of extra-virgin olive oil

4 to 6 cloves of garlic, chopped

¼ to ½ teaspoon of red pepper flakes

Bring a large pot of water to a boil and add the salt. Add the chicory, and then lower the heat to a simmer. Cook until the chicory is completely tender, 15 to 20 minutes. (If using spinach or Swiss chard, then just wilt until tender and cooked through, about 5 minutes.)

Drain, and when cool enough to handle, squeeze the water completely out of the greens.

Pour the olive oil into a large frying pan over medium heat and stir in the garlic and red pepper. When the garlic begins to sizzle, after about 1 minute but before it turns brown, add the greens and ½ cup of water to the pan. Cook, stirring, until the water has evaporated, about 5 minutes. Serve warm or at room temperature.

Crostata

JAM TART

Crostata is my go-to dessert for entertaining in Umbria. I've made it so many times, in so many versions, that guests sort of expect it at this point. The dough is a short crust, so the tart is basically like one big cookie. And what makes it so good is that it's extremely buttery. Although the recipe below is for all-purpose flour, I've been making it lately with stone-ground whole wheat flour, which gives the crust a more complex, nutty flavor.

The flavor of the jam is up to you. If you have a jar of homemade, even better. I collect homemade jams, whenever I see them in farmers' markets, so that I always have some on hand to whip up a last-minute dessert. Cherry and raspberry tend to be my favorites. **SERVES 8**

1½ cups of all-purpose or whole wheat flour

7 tablespoons of unsalted butter, at room temperature

2 large egg yolks, at room temperature

½ cup of sugar

Grated zest of 1 organic, unsprayed lemon (if using a conventional lemon, scrub it well and dry it)

Pinch of sea salt

About 1 cup of jam

Preheat the oven to 350°F.

Put the flour in a large bowl and make a well in the center. Add the butter, egg yolks, sugar, zest, and salt to the well. Mix the wet ingredients with your fingers, then slowly start mixing in the flour. Just use your fingers, and eventually the heel of your hand, to mush it all together until it forms a ball. This should only take a few minutes.

Let the dough rest for 10 minutes, covered with plastic wrap.

Line a 10-inch round tart pan with a removable rim with parchment paper. Place the dough in the tart pan. Don't try to roll it out, just spread it out to the edges with the palm of your hand to form an even crust.

Spread the jam evenly over the crust with the back of a spoon. Place the pan on the middle rack of the oven and bake for 20 to 25 minutes, until the jam is bubbling and the crust is golden. Let it cool completely before serving.

PANINI PARTY
IN UMBRIA

While most of the menus in this book are based on traditional ways of eating in Italy, this chapter is a bit different. Yes, it is *inspired* by tradition, location, and local ingredients, but the result is a way of entertaining—and eating—that is neither 100 percent Italian nor 100 percent American, but rather something in between.

Nancy Silverton is a chef who has had an intimate relationship with both bread and Italy for a long time. Her La Brea Bakery set the standard for a good loaf and introduced sourdough and artisanal bread to Los Angeles in the late 1980s. Her Mozza restaurants in LA take Italian cooking and ingredients and present them in creative and delicious ways. But her connections to Italy run way deeper than simple recipe creation. She has called a small town in Umbria home for at least part of every summer for the last fifteen years. With friends and family on a constant rotation around the large rustic table that is the beating heart of her home, she has developed ways to take advantage of local ingredients and traditions, while putting her own unmistakable stamp on things.

In her kitchen in Umbria Nancy brings home her station at Osteria Mozza's mozzarella bar. There mozzarella is her muse, as she creates small plates pairing the milky-white cheese with condiments, vegetables, and—of course—bread. Although mozzarella remains in her repertoire in Italy, she also brings in whatever happens to be in season or whatever grabs her attention at the market. The combinations come out of a career spent putting ingredients and tastes together.

The first time I arrived at Nancy's for lunch, I was met with tiny plates full of things like roasted peppers, sautéed radicchio, and slow-dried tomatoes. Once Nancy announced that we were just having panini, I assumed that this was going to be some sort of fantastical "make your own" kind of event. I should have known better. The small plates were simply Nancy's palette from which she would create tiny works of art in the form of perfectly made open-faced sandwiches.

While all of the ingredients were definitely Italian, the concept of an open-faced sandwich is not. We have bruschette and crostini in Italy, but this is neither.

Since a loaf of bread was to be the basis of our entire meal, I naturally assumed that Nancy, one of the queens of bread baking in the USA, would have made her own loaf. "Too much trouble." Instead she painstakingly canvased the bakeries in her town until she found a loaf that met her high standards and was suited to carrying her toppings. A crust that was firm but not too hard to bite into. A crumb that was springy but not full of air holes that would let the toppings fall through.

I've since had the pleasure of watching Nancy create these mini masterpieces several times. They are never quite the same, and watching her work is like watching an artist in her studio. A bit of this, a bit of that, but every single "this" and "that" well thought out and sourced. The result is gorgeous, creative, and delicious—a way of entertaining that I have copied and adopted many times over.

Recipe for a Party

Turning this menu into a party is like creating a work of art on your table. The sandwiches themselves are mini masterpieces, and together they sing color, texture, and taste that explode in abundant variations. Although I've supplied five recipes, don't think of them as carved in stone. Instead, do as Nancy does, and be inspired by the season, and the hues, to craft your own.

menu

Antipasto

Crostini di Olive
TAPENADE TOAST 205

Panini

Bagna Cauda Toast with Radicchio, Egg, and Anchovies 208

Finocchiona and Roasted Pepper Panino 210

Mozzarella, Tomato, Arugula, and Pesto Panino 212

Ricotta with Mint, Eggplant, and Roasted Tomato Panino 213

Dolce

Uva al Forno
ROASTED GRAPES 215

what to drink

WINE

Although everything can be eaten at once with red wine, if you'd like to turn the Tapenade Toast into something to go with an aperitivo, then a chilled light white wine would be perfect. Think crisp and just a tad fruity, like one of the new generation of Verdicchio wines from the Marche region.

At any time of year these rustic sandwiches go with an easy red—nothing too fruity or too tannic. A Montefalco Rosso—a blend of Sangiovese, a bit of Sagrantino, and Merlot or Cabernet Sauvignon—complements the food. An alternative would be a Montepulciano d'Abruzzo. Don't bother with before- or after-dinner drinks with this meal. It's meant to be casual and easy. Just make sure you have enough wine!

timing

Much of the work of this menu comes in the shopping end of things, so do take some time to source your ingredients well. The most important homework is finding the right loaf of bread and deciding how to toast it. If you are going to prepare this menu for guests, then I strongly suggest you have a dry run with a simple sandwich (tomato and mozzarella, for example) to make sure your bread works and that you have a way to toast it that you're comfortable with. Most of the toppings can be prepared the day before. Just make sure you bring them back to room temperature before assembling and serving your panini.

1 DAY BEFORE

Prepare and refrigerate the following toppings:

Radicchio
Hard-boiled eggs
Roasted peppers
Fried eggplant
Tapenade

THE MORNING OF YOUR DINNER

Buy the bread.

3 HOURS BEFORE

Take all of the ingredients out of the refrigerator (prepared ingredients as well as cheese and meat).

Roast the grapes.

Set the table.

1 HOUR BEFORE

Toast the bread for the panini.

½ HOUR BEFORE

Toast the bread for the tapenade, and set that out for guests.

These panini are best eaten soon after they are made, so while guests munch on the tapenade, you can start to assemble the panini.

inspiration

SET YOUR TABLE

Nancy sets a very casual table in Italy. Her long wooden table is in the middle of a room that acts as entrance hall, kitchen, and dining room. It is the boisterous, happy, busy beating heart of her house.

TABLEWARE

The table that Nancy sets is the happy place somewhere between a buffet and sit-down. Stacks of heavy white plates (food always looks good on them) mix with a jumble of flea market–find silverware tumbled across the table.

As you assemble the panini, settle them carefully onto heavy serving boards. Nancy has a large collection of stunning boards made of olive wood, in varying shapes. The open-faced sandwiches are laid on top, ready to be portioned into three or four pieces with Nancy's sharpest chef's knife. But wait to cut them until guests sit down: they look so pretty untouched.

GLASSWARE

Stacks of chunky tumblers are for wine, water, or both.

EXTRAS

A centerpiece usually features a vase full of wildflowers.

Crostini di Olive

TAPENADE TOAST

This olive spread on bread is more of an antipasto than a panino. And while Nancy calls it by its French name, *tapenade, pate di olive* is also common in Italy. Nancy puts her own California spin on things with the addition of both orange and lemon zest, which definitely make the taste brighter (not to mention irresistible).

Use a small baguette-type loaf for this, something that will give you a higher crust-to-crumb ratio, a ciabatta, or even a whole wheat baguette. MAKES 16 CROSTINI

2 tablespoons of capers

1½ cups of pitted taggiasche or similar intense black olives

⅓ cup of extra-virgin olive oil

4 or 5 anchovy fillets

Grated zest of 1 organic, unsprayed orange (if using a conventional orange, scrub it well and dry it)

Grated zest of 1 organic, unsprayed lemon (if using a conventional lemon, scrub it well and dry it)

1 or more tablespoons of freshly squeezed lemon juice

1 clove of garlic, peeled

1 baguette or ciabatta loaf

¼ cup of chopped Italian flat-leaf parsley

If using capers packed in salt, place them in a small bowl and cover with water to soak for 15 minutes before rinsing and draining.

To make the tapenade, place 1 cup of the olives in a food processor and process until roughly chopped. Add the olive oil, anchovies, capers, half of the orange and lemon zests, and 1 tablespoon lemon juice. Grate in the garlic clove using a Microplane, or use a garlic press, and process until smooth. Transfer to a small bowl.

Roughly chop the rest of the olives and add them to the mixture. Stir well and taste. Add more lemon juice if desired. (If making ahead, store in an airtight container in the refrigerator and let come to room temperature before serving.)

Cut the bread into sixteen ¼-inch-thick slices and toast it. Spread a thin layer of the tapenade on each slice. Top each with some of the rest of the orange and lemon zest and some parsley.

Panini

OPEN-FACED SANDWICHES

Once you get the hang of these sandwiches (basically toasting, seasoning, and topping the bread), you can play around with other ingredients and toppings. Be inspired by the season: if it's not summer, then forget about the tomato and mozzarella one. Think about color and texture and how they will work together. But do remember to stick to the three-ingredient rule: never pile on the toppings.

Each of these recipes makes four open-faced sandwiches. When figuring out quantities for your party, count on two pieces of bread per person. If you make this entire menu you will have enough for at least ten guests.

One of the seemingly simple things I picked up from Nancy (she is a chef, after all) is the importance of seasoning each layer. The bread always needs it, as do any vegetable toppings you use. Although adding salt and pepper (and oil and vinegar and any other condiments) might usually seem an afterthought, when Nancy starts fashioning these panini, the seasonings play a crucial role.

Each of the open-faced sandwiches is meant to be shared. You'll be presenting them on a thick wooden serving board (see pages 198–99) and they can and should be cut into at least two if not four separate pieces. **EACH RECIPE MAKES 4 PANINI**

A word about toasting: Nancy uses a professional panini press in her kitchen in Umbria, which works wonders, getting super hot and leaving professional-looking grill marks. If you have a panini press, then by all means use it. If not? Don't worry. For the recipes in which you have to oil the bread first, you can either use a ridged grill pan with a weight on top of the bread or else the broiler (but be careful not to burn your bread). For the bread that does not get brushed with oil before toasting, a regular toaster or toaster oven will do just fine.

{ *continues* }

Bagna Cauda Toast with Radicchio, Egg, and Anchovies

Bagna cauda is almost like a vegetable fondue. In the region of Piemonte, a pot of melted butter, olive oil, garlic, and anchovies is put in the center of the table and guests dip raw vegetables like fennel, carrots, and celery in it. Nancy uses the same intense oil mixture, but instead douses toasted bread with it to form the basis of a radicchio panino.

FOR THE RADICCHIO

3 tablespoons of extra-virgin olive oil, plus more for drizzling

1 tablespoon of Aceto Balsamico di Modena

2 teaspoons of fresh rosemary leaves

1 small head of radicchio, separated into leaves

FOR THE BAGNA CAUDA

⅓ cup of extra-virgin olive oil

3 tablespoons of unsalted butter

⅛ teaspoon of red pepper flakes

4 anchovy fillets

2 cloves of garlic, crushed or grated

———

2 slices of rustic country bread

3 hard-boiled eggs, cooled, peeled, and sliced

6 to 8 anchovy fillets

Chopped fresh Italian flat-leaf parsley, for garnish

Fleur de sel or other flaky finishing salt

To prepare the radicchio: Put the olive oil, balsamic vinegar, and rosemary in a blender and blend to mix. Put the radicchio in a medium bowl, pour over the dressing, toss to coat the leaves with the mixture, and let sit for 20 minutes, until wilted.

Put the radicchio and dressing in a nonstick frying pan over medium-high heat and cook for just 2 minutes to completely wilt the leaves. Remove from the heat and set aside to cool completely.

To prepare the bagna cauda: Put the olive oil and butter in a small frying pan. Heat over medium until the butter melts. Add the red pepper flakes, anchovies, and garlic, stirring so the anchovies dissolve and the garlic becomes fragrant. Remove from the heat.

Toast the bread using either a panini press or a grill pan, or under the broiler. When the bread is evenly toasted, remove from the heat.

To assemble the panini: Using a spoon, drizzle each slice of bread liberally with the bagna cauda. Place a few radicchio leaves on top of each slice of bread. Cover the radicchio with egg slices (a little more than 1 egg per slice of bread). Gently layer several anchovies on top of the eggs, scatter with parsley and salt, and drizzle with olive oil.

Place on a wooden serving board. Using a sharp knife, slice each panino into three or four pieces, and serve.

Finocchiona and Roasted Pepper Panino

Roasting the peppers for this panino is probably the most time-consuming step in this menu. But cooking them until charred, and then rubbing the skins off, leads to that magical combination of both sweet and smoky that defines this panino and pairs perfectly with the fennel-scented salami. Finocchiona is one of the most common types of salami you'll find in Tuscany, where wild fennel (*finocchio*) grows right by the side of the road. Finocchiona is fatty and rich and its flavor is unique (which a garnish of fresh dill, in particular, brings out). If you can't find it, substitute whatever other high-quality salami you can find. The trick is to ask your butcher to slice it thinly, so that it is easy to bite.

(pictured opposite, bottom left)

1 pound of red bell peppers

Four ½-inch-thick slices of rustic country Italian bread

About ½ cup of extra-virgin olive oil, for toasting and drizzling

1 clove of garlic, peeled

¼ pound of thinly sliced finocchiona or other fennel salami

Fresh dill fronds (preferred) or basil leaves, for garnish

Fleur de sel or other flaky finishing salt

Preheat the oven to 500°F.

Place the whole peppers on a baking sheet. Roast for 30 to 40 minutes, turning them about halfway through, until the peppers look wrinkled and collapsed and slightly charred. Remove them from the oven and cover them tightly with aluminum foil. Let them rest for about a half hour.

Once cool enough to handle, use paper towels to rub off and discard the skin, then cut the peppers into quarters, removing the stems, ribs, and seeds. Put the peppers in a small bowl.

Brush both sides of the bread slices with olive oil. Toast using either a panini press or a grill pan, or under the broiler. When the bread is evenly toasted, remove from the heat and rub one side with garlic.

To assemble the panini: Set the bread on a cutting board and top it with the sliced salami, folding it in half to give it some height. Layer some of the red peppers on top, then garnish with fresh dill. Finish with a sprinkle of flaky salt and a drizzle of olive oil.

Place on a wooden serving board. Using a sharp knife, slice each panino into three or four pieces, and serve.

Mozzarella, Tomato, Arugula, and Pesto Panino

We can agree that we all love both pesto and caprese salad, right? Then this recipe, which is the panino version of both of those combined, is going to please everyone.

Fair warning: if you can't find great ripe tomatoes and fantastically fresh mozzarella, then skip to the next panino. This one is all about the ingredients.

(pictured page 211, top)

FOR THE PESTO

1 large bunch of fresh basil, leaves only

1 clove of garlic, peeled

Grated zest of ½ organic, unsprayed lemon (if using a conventional lemon, scrub it well and dry it)

¼ cup of pine nuts

½ cup of extra-virgin olive oil

1 ounce of Parmigiano-Reggiano, grated (¼ cup)

Sea salt

FOR THE PANINI

3 cups of arugula leaves, rinsed and dried

2 tablespoons of extra-virgin olive oil, plus more for brushing the bread

1 tablespoon of freshly squeezed lemon juice

Sea salt

½ pound of fresh mozzarella

3 ripe tomatoes

Four ½-inch-thick slices of rustic Italian bread

1 clove of garlic, peeled

To make the pesto: Place the basil in either a food processor or mortar and add the garlic, lemon zest, and pine nuts. With the motor running (or while grinding with a pestle), drizzle in the olive oil. Transfer to a small bowl and stir in the Parmigiano. Taste and adjust for salt.

To assemble the panini: Put the arugula in a medium bowl and dress with the olive oil, lemon juice, and salt to taste.

Cut the mozzarella into ⅓-inch-thick slices and let drain for 10 minutes in a sieve over a bowl.

Cut the tomatoes into ⅓-inch-thick slices.

Brush both sides of the bread slices with olive oil. Toast using either a panini press or grill pan, or under the broiler. When the bread is evenly toasted, remove from the heat and rub one side with the garlic.

Set the bread on a cutting board and layer each piece with some arugula. Place 2 slices of tomato on each piece of bread, side by side. Top each tomato with a slice of mozzarella and drizzle liberally with the pesto.

Place on a wooden serving board. Using a sharp knife, slice each panino into three or four pieces, and serve.

Ricotta with Mint, Eggplant, and Roasted Tomato Panino

This is Nancy's panino version of pasta alla Norma, a Sicilian dish that combines fried eggplant with tomatoes and ricotta salata over pasta. Slow-roasting the cherry tomatoes, and then carefully layering the ingredients, stacks up to a luscious—and filling—sandwich.

To keep the eggplant from turning out too heavy, make sure you use enough oil to fry it in, and that it is hot enough. Otherwise, the eggplant will absorb too much oil.

(pictured page 211, bottom right)

½ pound of cherry or grape tomatoes

Sea salt and freshly ground black pepper

Extra-virgin olive oil

½ pound of eggplant

1½ cups of fresh ricotta

Four ½-inch-thick slices of rustic Italian bread

1 clove of garlic, peeled

1 cup of fresh mint leaves, plus more for garnish

4 ounces of ricotta salata, grated (½ cup)

Preheat the oven to 450°F.

Cut the tomatoes in half and arrange them in one layer on a rimmed baking sheet or in a shallow baking dish. Season them with salt to taste and a generous drizzle of extra-virgin olive oil. Roast for about 30 minutes, until they have begun to dry out. Remove from the oven and let cool. Place in a bowl and set aside.

Cut the eggplant into ½-inch-thick rounds. Using a sharp knife, score across the surface of each slice on one side.

Line a large plate with paper towels. Pour the olive oil into a large frying pan to a depth of ½ inch and heat on medium-high until hot. (A drop of water will sizzle in the oil.) Add one layer of eggplant and cook, turning once, until completely tender, about 10 minutes total. Remove from the oil with a slotted spoon and transfer to the paper towels to drain. Repeat with the rest of the eggplant.

Place the fresh ricotta in a small bowl and whip with a fork until smooth.

To assemble the panini: Brush both sides of the bread slices with olive oil. Toast using either a panini press or grill pan, or under the broiler. When the bread is evenly toasted, remove from the heat and rub one side with the garlic.

Cut the mint leaves into ribbons. Cover each piece of bread with ¼ inch or so of the fresh ricotta and then sprinkle with the mint. Drizzle with olive oil. Lay 2 slices of eggplant on top of each piece of bread and top with roasted tomatoes. Sprinkle with the grated ricotta salata and garnish with whole mint leaves. Season with salt and pepper.

Place on a wooden serving board. Using a sharp knife, slice each panino into three or four pieces, and serve.

Uva al Forno

ROASTED GRAPES

This is barely a recipe but makes the perfect ending to this panini extravaganza. After all the bread, guests probably won't want any sort of cake or pie, but fruit is very welcome. Roasting the grapes, which condenses their juices so they're almost like candy, makes them more indulgent, instead of like a good-for-you kind of fruit dessert.

Serve them by simply placing them on the prettiest platter you have. The different shades of fruit, glistening under their own syrup, look divine. You can serve them with cheese if you like—but the grapes are fantastic enough on their own. **SERVES 6**

2 or 3 bunches of dark grapes (about 1½ pounds)

Preheat the oven to 350°F.

Place the bunches of grapes on a baking sheet without crowding them. Roast them for at least 45 minutes or up to an hour and 15 minutes. It's difficult to time them, since grape sizes differ. They are done when they start to blister and have shrunken to about one-third of their original size. If you're roasting several different types of grapes, they will probably cook differently, so keep an eye on them.

When they're done, remove the sheet from the oven, and let cool to room temperature. Carefully remove the grapes from the baking sheet, and arrange them on a pretty platter or wooden serving board.

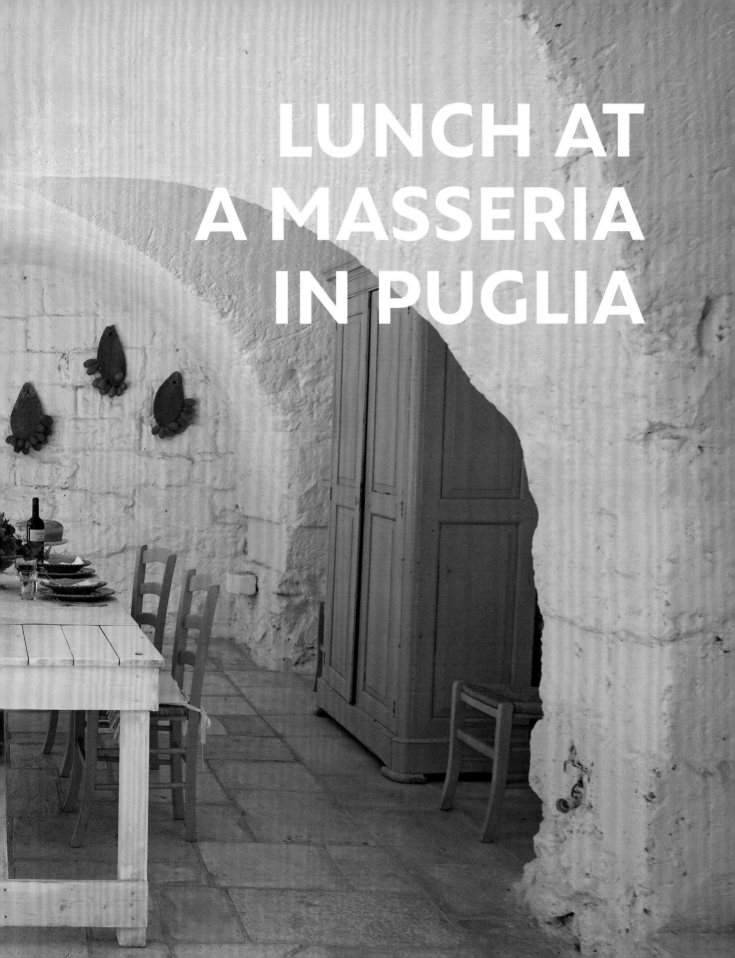

LUNCH AT A MASSERIA IN PUGLIA

One of the many charms of Italy is that it remains, even in the twenty-first century, an intensely agricultural country. While the cities are crowded, the countryside—dotted with stone houses and fields of vines, olive trees, and other crops—is usually just a short drive away. But that's not to say that everything remains frozen in time. While the crops may remain unchanged, the stone houses that used to be home to the men and women who worked the fields have undergone sweeping changes in the last decades.

If you've read *Under the Tuscan Sun* (and who hasn't?) then you probably know where I'm going. Farm buildings that used to be inhabited by laborers in the system of *mezzadria* (which was basically serfdom) began to crumble and fall to ruin when this system was abolished in the twentieth century. Fieldwork became more mechanized, farmers moved into more urban areas, and fewer people were needed to tend the crops.

I've written four books about restoring these abandoned structures and turning them into warm and inviting homes, and have even restored my own with my husband, Domenico, who has made a career out of this kind of architectural work. Over the last two decades, many of the crumbling ruins dotting the central Italian landscape have been bought, restored, and given a new, different lease on life.

It's only recently, though, as charming ruins became harder (and more expensive) to find in regions like Tuscany, that people started looking farther south, exploring regions like Puglia, Sicily, and Abruzzo.

Puglia is the most recent region to go through this transformation. If ten years ago there was nowhere to stay, nowadays the number of truly beautiful and unique hotels located in formerly abandoned estates is hard to choose from.

One of the most charming is Masseria Potenti, an estate that was lovingly brought back to life by the Tommasino family. Originally from Puglia, they moved to Milan thirty years ago, but always hoped to return. When they first saw Masseria Potenti, their dream was to restore it as their private home, and as a place to be able to invite all the friends they had made in the north of Italy to discover their family's southern roots.

Masserias are rural structures that exist only in the south of Italy, particularly in Puglia. Usually quite large, each structure was the center of an estate that housed not only the landowners, but the workers who tended the crops and the animals and equipment as well. In other words, they are massive, and as the Tommasino family soon realized, their masseria was too much house for them to use themselves. And so they transformed it into a hotel, where they still live, but also receive guests.

Maria Grazia Tommasino, the wife and mother of the family, has an incredible sense of taste, style, and drama that she brings with her into the kitchen, transforming simple ingredients into uniquely beautiful, yet unfussy, feasts.

Recipe for a Party

Maria Grazia and her daughter, Chiara, are the kind of hostesses who just keep bringing out more food. It is a completely southern thing that is in their genes. Meals in the south of Italy go on forever, which is not a bad way to live life.

If you want, feel free to cut this menu back to just two courses of your choice. But even if this menu seems like a lot of food, the beauty is that except for the fish, it's all vegetarian, and so it's actually very light.

menu

Aperitivi

Friselle con Pomodorini
RUSKS WITH TOMATOES 222

Crostini con Ricotta e Marmellata di Peperoncino
CROSTINI WITH RICOTTA AND HOT PEPPER JAM 224

{*Pane*—Crusty Italian Bread}

Antipasto

Rotolini di Zucchini con Ricotta
RICOTTA-STUFFED ZUCCHINI 227

Primo

Pasta con Pomodorini Schiacciati e Rughetta
PASTA WITH SMASHED CHERRY TOMATOES AND ARUGULA 228

Secondo

Sformato di Pesce con Verdura
FISH AND VEGETABLE TERRINE 230

Dolci

Torta di Fichi
FIG CAKE 233

what to drink

WINE

Pugliese wines have undergone a renaissance recently; Masseria Potenti produces and serves their own. Before rosé became so trendy, it was always popular in Puglia, and now almost everyone produces it. Usually made from the Negroamaro grape, the rosé from this region is bright, crisp, and not too fruity—a perfect choice for a summer menu.

The most famous red wine from Puglia is Primitivo. It is the name of both the grape and the wine. These wines tend to be very dark and joyfully fruity. The name Primitivo actually refers to the fact that the grapes ripen early. Once ripe, they have a lot of sugar, yet since they ripen unevenly, there are usually green, unripe grapes in the bunches as well, which balances out the wine and prevents it from being too sweet.

timing

1 DAY BEFORE

Bake the Fig Cake.

Bake the Friselle (if making your own).

Cook the vegetables for the antipasto and the Fish and Vegetable Terrine.

Place the fish and vegetables in the loaf pan for the Fish and Vegetable Terrine and refrigerate.

Chill the wine.

2 HOURS BEFORE

Remove the vegetables from the refrigerator to bring to room temperature.

Set the table.

1 HOUR BEFORE

Prepare all the ingredients for the pasta sauce.

Unmold the Fish and Vegetable Terrine.

Prepare the antipasto.

20 MINUTES BEFORE YOUR GUESTS ARRIVE

Prepare the aperitivi snacks.

inspiration

SET YOUR TABLE

Maria Grazia and Chiara's outgoing and vibrant personalities are perfectly reflected in every aspect of the way they entertain. Against the blindingly white backdrop of the masseria in the full sun, they set tables that are full of bold color and surprising contrasts.

DRESSING YOUR TABLE

A handwoven piece of linen from her collection of textiles, strewn across the center of the table, acts as a sort of runner.

TABLEWARE AND UTENSILS

Her set of turquoise-colored plates, from Grottaglie, are handmade by nearby artisans. In addition to plates, Maria Grazia uses a footed fruit bowl, a pitcher, and a ceramic pine cone (a good-luck talisman) to add height. Chiara is in charge of the centerpiece, mixing flowers with grapes cut from the nearby pergola.

Her flatware has been collected over the years.

GLASSWARE

Maria Grazia doesn't believe in too much matching, so she uses an array of vintage glasses to animate the table even further.

Friselle con Pomodorini

RUSKS WITH TOMATOES

Friselle come in all shapes and sizes all over the south of Italy. Made from twice-baked bread, this hard rusk or cracker provides a great base for vegetables (usually chopped tomatoes), and works well crumbled into soups to thicken otherwise thin broths. Previously a frugal way of preserving bread, today it has escaped the role of cucina povera.

While most people simply buy their friselle already made, Maria Grazia likes making hers. Most friselle are about 4 inches in diameter, but these mini ones are perfect for topping with almost anything at aperitivo time. This recipe makes more than you need, and any leftover friselle will last for months in an airtight container or bag. **MAKES 48 FRISELLE; SERVES 6 AS AN APERITIVO, WITH LEFTOVER FRISELLE**

For the friselle

2 teaspoons of active dry yeast

2 cups lukewarm water

2 tablespoons of extra-virgin olive oil, plus more for oiling the bowl

3⅓ cups of bread flour (preferably hard durum wheat)

¼ teaspoon of sea salt

For the topping

2 ripe medium tomatoes

4 or 5 fresh basil leaves

2 to 3 tablespoons of extra-virgin olive oil

½ teaspoon of sea salt

To make the friselle: Add the yeast to the water in a small bowl and let it dissolve.

Prepare a lightly oiled large bowl.

Mound the flour on a work surface. Once the yeast has dissolved, make a well in the middle of the flour and add the water with the yeast, olive oil, and salt. Using your hands, begin to work the flour into the water. Once all the liquid is incorporated, knead the dough until smooth and springy to the touch, about 10 minutes. Transfer it to the oiled bowl and cover it with a clean dish towel. Let it rise for 1½ hours, until about doubled in size.

Transfer the dough to a work surface. Punch it down and knead it for a few minutes until it is compact and springy. Break off a small piece of dough, about walnut-sized. Roll it into a rope measuring 3 inches long and ¾ inch in diameter. Connect the ends, making a small doughnut shape. Repeat with the rest of the dough. (You should end up with about 24 rings.) Place them on a baking sheet, spaced 2 inches apart, and let them rise, covered again with a clean dish towel, for another hour.

In the meantime, preheat the oven to 350°F.

Bake the friselle for 40 minutes, until slightly golden.

Remove them from the oven and cut each round of bread in half, into two rounds. Place them cut side up on the baking sheet, return to the oven, and continue baking until they are golden, dry, and crisp, another 20 to 30 minutes. Remove them from the oven and let cool completely.

To make the topping: Core and chop the tomatoes into a small dice and place them in a medium bowl. Tear the basil into small pieces and add to the bowl, along with the olive oil and salt. Stir to combine and let it rest for 10 to 20 minutes.

Place 12 of the friselle on a pretty platter and spoon some of the tomatoes on top of each one, along with some of the juices from the bowl. Let sit for 10 minutes before serving, to allow the friselle to soften a bit.

Crostini con Ricotta e Marmellata di Peperoncino

CROSTINI WITH RICOTTA AND HOT PEPPER JAM

Maria Grazia and Chiara love using the produce they grow on the estate in cooking as well as decoration. One of the most glorious things they make are wreaths crafted out of bright hot red peppers. These "crowns" are hung all over the masseria, and grace the tables as centerpieces. As they dry out the vivid red becomes a deep magenta, until the peppers are completely dried, and then used in the kitchen. But while they are still fresh, the family makes huge batches of hot pepper jam.

Maria Grazia goes all out with these little snacks. The homemade jam pairs with ricotta that comes from her flock of sheep. Feel free to buy your bread already made—and because I'm pretty sure you don't raise sheep, you can also buy the ricotta. While there are pretty good hot pepper jams available these days, here I'm going to suggest that you make your own. It's beyond easy and if you put it up in little jars (as Maria Grazia does), they make wonderful gifts. It pairs well with fresh, tangy cheeses like goat or cream cheese, or can be used in sandwiches with stronger sheep's milk cheeses or even Swiss cheese. SERVES 6; MAKES 1 CUP OF JAM

For the jam

1⅔ to 2½ cups (7 ounces) of small, hot fresh red chile peppers, stemmed (see Note, opposite)

½ cup (3½ ounces) of sugar

———

1 cup of fresh ricotta (preferably sheep's milk)

3 slices of dark whole-grain bread

12 to 24 fresh mint leaves, for garnish

To make the jam: Put the chile peppers and sugar in a food processor and process until the peppers are completely chopped. Transfer the mixture to a small, thick-bottomed pot and cook over medium heat for about 35 minutes, until somewhat thickened. Pour the jam into small sterilized jars and seal them.

To assemble the crostini: Put the ricotta in a small bowl, and using a fork, whip it until smooth.

Cut each slice of bread into four squares. Top each square of bread with about 1 teaspoon of the ricotta and about ¼ teaspoon of the jam. Top each crostino with a mint leaf or two and serve.

NOTE Be very careful when dealing with hot peppers. Stand away from the food processor when opening it up after processing, and be especially wary of sticking your head above the pot while the jam is cooking. It's important to avoid breathing in the fumes from fresh hot red peppers.

Rotolini di Zucchini con Ricotta

RICOTTA-STUFFED ZUCCHINI

This elegant little antipasto couldn't be easier. Although Maria Grazia uses ricotta, I've made it often with goat cheese. It's the perfect starter during summer, when zucchini are at their best, and the addition of mint and poppy seeds not only adds texture and flavor, but also creates a pretty contrast to the whiteness of the ricotta. SERVES 4 TO 6

4 medium zucchini, trimmed

2 tablespoons of extra-virgin olive oil

1 bunch of fresh mint, leaves only

Sea salt

1½ cups of fresh ricotta

½ cup of poppy seeds

Fresh sage or basil leaves, for garnish

Extra-virgin olive oil, for drizzling (preferably your best variety)

Preheat the oven to 350°F.

Using a sharp knife or mandoline, cut the zucchini lengthwise into ⅛-inch-thick ribbons. (You should end up with at least 12 full-length, unbroken ribbons.) Place the zucchini in one layer on one or two baking sheets. Season them with 1 tablespoon of the olive oil, half of the mint, and salt to taste and bake them for about 10 minutes, until just tender. Remove from the oven and let cool completely.

In the meantime, place the ricotta in a medium bowl with the remaining tablespoon of olive oil and the rest of the mint, roughly chopped. Using a fork, whip it until smooth and creamy.

Place about 2 tablespoons of the ricotta mixture on each strip of zucchini and roll it up. Place the poppy seeds in a shallow bowl. Dip both flat ends of the rolls in the poppy seeds, coating the ricotta.

To serve, place two or three rolls on individual plates. Garnish each roll by placing a sage or basil leaf on top and tucking the ends in so that it follows the curve of the roll. Drizzle with your best extra-virgin olive oil and serve.

Pasta con Pomodorini Schiacciati e Rughetta

PASTA WITH SMASHED CHERRY TOMATOES AND ARUGULA

This is one of those effortless recipes that relies on extraordinary ingredients. The cherry tomatoes used here are *datterini*, a particularly intense variety grown on the estate. If you're unsure if your cherry tomatoes are up to the job, just taste one. If it's watery and bland, this recipe won't do anything to improve it. Better to move on to another recipe or else search out better tomatoes.

The arugula used here is the perennial variety, which grows wild in Puglia. Tough and spicy, it adds both flavor and texture to the dish. Prewashed, bagged hothouse arugula may not have the same effect but will be close. **SERVES 6**

Sea salt and freshly ground black pepper

1 pound of cavatelli or orecchiette

⅓ cup of extra-virgin olive oil, plus more for drizzling

1 pound of cherry tomatoes

¼ cup of fresh basil leaves

1 bunch of arugula or other spicy green, rinsed and dried

4 ounces of ricotta salata, grated (1 cup)

Bring a large pot of salted water to boil. Add the pasta and cook according to the package directions until al dente.

In the meantime, pour the olive oil into a large frying pan (big enough to hold the drained pasta later). Add the cherry tomatoes, basil, and salt and pepper to taste. Cook over high heat for about 10 minutes, until the tomatoes have started to break down.

Drain the pasta and add it to the tomatoes. Using the back of your spoon, smash the tomatoes to let their juices run out. Toss well to coat the pasta completely.

Divide the pasta into six individual bowls. Scatter the arugula leaves and ricotta salata over the top. Drizzle with more olive oil and serve immediately.

Sformato di Pesce con Verdura

FISH AND VEGETABLE TERRINE

This recipe is further evidence that much of the cooking in Puglia is about letting vegetables just do their thing. Here, they get paired with fish and candied lemons, resulting in an elegant—and light—main course. SERVES 6 TO 8

3 tablespoons of capers

2 pounds of branzino or sea bass fillets (skin on if possible)

Extra-virgin olive oil

Sea salt and freshly ground black pepper

5 small eggplants (about 1 pound), trimmed and cut lengthwise into ½-inch-wide strips

4 red bell peppers, seeded, ribs removed, and cut into ½-inch-wide strips

6 medium zucchini, cut lengthwise into ½-inch-wide strips

1 medium red onion, cut into ½-inch-thick rings

½ pound of cherry tomatoes

2 teaspoons of dried oregano

2 organic, unsprayed lemons (if using conventional lemons, scrub them well and dry them)

2 to 3 tablespoons of light brown sugar

Preheat the oven to 350°F.

If using capers packed in salt, place them in a small bowl and cover with water to soak for 15 minutes before rinsing and draining.

Place the fish fillets on an oiled baking sheet in one layer, skin side down. Drizzle them with olive oil and season with salt and pepper. Bake for 8 minutes, until opaque. Remove from the oven and let cool. Leave the oven on at 350°F.

Place the eggplants, peppers, zucchini, onions, and cherry tomatoes on two oiled baking sheets. Drizzle with olive oil and season with salt, pepper, and the oregano. Toss with the capers. Bake until tender, about 25 minutes. Remove from the oven and let cool. Keep the oven on at 350°F.

Cover a clean baking sheet with parchment paper. Cut 1 of the lemons into very thin slices (⅛ inch). Place them on the parchment and sprinkle with the brown sugar. Bake for 20 minutes, until just starting to go golden Remove from the oven and let cool, then chop into a small dice.

Line a 9 by 5-inch loaf pan with plastic wrap. Place the fish fillets at the bottom of the pan, skin side down, then layer a mix of the vegetables, adding some of the caramelized lemons as you go, and pressing down after each layer so that everything will adhere.

After the loaf pan is filled, cover it with plastic wrap and place it in the refrigerator for at least 2 hours to firm up.

Remove from the refrigerator, uncover it, and turn the terrine onto a serving platter. Let it come to room temperature.

In the meantime, grate the zest of the remaining lemon. Sprinkle the terrine with the zest. Cut the zested lemon in half and squeeze a bit of lemon juice over the terrine. Drizzle with olive oil and serve.

Torta di Fichi

FIG CAKE

This fruit-topped cake, in various versions, shows up almost every morning for breakfast at Masseria Potenti. Apricots, peaches, apples, and pears all make their appearance. The most decadently delicious version, though, is the one made with ripe figs. Needless to say, in addition to breakfast, it's also sublime for dessert—and whenever else you want to eat it during the day. MAKES ONE 9-INCH CAKE; SERVES 6 TO 8

¾ cup (1½ sticks) of unsalted butter, at room temperature

1 cup of granulated sugar

4 large eggs, at room temperature

¼ cup of whole milk

2 cups of all-purpose flour

2½ teaspoons of baking powder

¼ teaspoon of sea salt

¼ cup of confectioners' sugar

1 pound of ripe fresh figs, halved from tip to bottom

Preheat the oven to 350°F.

Beat the butter and granulated sugar in a large bowl until light yellow and creamy, about 5 minutes. Add the eggs and milk and continue to beat until well combined.

Put the flour in a large bowl. Stir in the baking powder and salt. Stir the flour mixture, a bit at a time, into the egg mixture, until it is completely smooth and incorporated.

Line the bottom of a 9-inch springform cake pan with parchment paper. Pour in the batter. Put the confectioners' sugar in a small bowl. Roll each of the fig halves in the powdered sugar and then press them into the surface of the cake, cut side up.

Bake for about 30 minutes. A toothpick should come out clean when inserted into the center.

Remove from the oven and let cool completely before removing it from the pan. To remove, carefully run a knife along the inside edge of the pan to loosen the cake before removing the ring. Transfer the cake from the bottom of the pan to a serving platter.

CONVERSION CHART

All conversions are approximate.

LIQUID CONVERSIONS

U.S.	Metric
1 tsp	5 ml
1 tbs	15 ml
2 tbs	30 ml
3 tbs	45 ml
¼ cup	60 ml
⅓ cup	75 ml
⅓ cup + 1 tbs	90 ml
⅓ cup + 2 tbs	100 ml
½ cup	120 ml
⅔ cup	150 ml
¾ cup	180 ml
¾ cup + 2 tbs	200 ml
1 cup	240 ml
1 cup + 2tbs	275 ml
1¼ cups	300 ml
1⅓ cups	325 ml
1½ cups	350 ml
1⅔ cups	375 ml
1¾ cups	400 ml
1¾ cups + 2 tbs	450 ml
2 cups (1 pint)	475 ml
2½ cups	600 ml
3 cups	720 ml
4 cups (1 quart)	945 ml (1,000 ml is 1 liter)

WEIGHT CONVERSIONS

U.S./U.K.	Metric
½ oz	14 g
1 oz	28 g
1½ oz	43 g
2 oz	57 g
2½ oz	71 g
3 oz	85 g
3½ oz	100 g
4 oz	113 g
5 oz	142 g
6 oz	170 g
7 oz	200 g
8 oz	227 g
9 oz	255 g
10 oz	284 g
11 oz	312 g
12 oz	340 g
13 oz	368 g
14 oz	400 g
15 oz	425 g
1 lb	454 g

OVEN TEMPERATURES

°F	Gas Mark	°C
250	½	120
275	1	140
300	2	150
325	3	165
350	4	180
375	5	190
400	6	200
425	7	220
450	8	230
475	9	240
500	10	260
550	Broil	290

INDEX

(Page references in *italics* refer to illustrations.)

ACKNOWLEDGMENTS

The most difficult part of writing this book was the enjoyable task of looking at a lifetime of wonderful meals and being forced to choose just a handful to feature. So first of all, a heartfelt thank-you to everyone who has ever hosted me in their home or restaurant. I'm sorry I couldn't include every single meal, but please know that the things I learned—and ate— informed every word I wrote.

My biggest thanks goes to all of those who graciously let me document the meals I did choose, in both words and images. Mille grazie to: Pupetto Hotel and Gabriella Guida, the beach clubs Ferdinando and Grassi, Hotel San Pietro, and Da Adolfo in Positano; All'Arco, Cantinone gia' Schiavi, Do Mori, Alla Vedova, Do Colonne, and Mauro Stoppa in Venice; Alessandra Branca, Domenico Cortese, and Sofie Wochner in Rome; Rocco and his family at Trattoria Rocca in Florence; Fabrizia Lanza and Tasca D'Almerita in Sicily; Maria Grazia, Chiara, and the entire Tomassino family at Masseria Potenti; Claudia Ruspoli and Mirella Piccione at Castello Ruspoli, Vignanello; Nancy Silverton and Michael Krikorian in Umbria; Manuel and Massimliano Messina at Pizzeria Li Scalini in Rome; the owners and staff at La Selva in Ariccia; and Maria Chiara Passani and Simone Ficarelli at the Consorzio del Parmigiano-Reggiano, and Maria Elisa Piroli and Rina Pellegrini in Emilia-Romagna.

This book is only possible because my original editor, Christopher Steighner, said yes to a vague idea I had over lunch one day in New York. Heartfelt thanks to editor extraordinaire Aliza Fogelson for taking on this project late in the game. You took all the moving parts that I eventually handed in and turned them, with elegance and great style, into a book that is not only beautiful, but that is also useful. And many thanks to Tricia Levi for jumping in at the very end, to see this book to press and for the perfect subtitle!

Many thanks to the design team at Rizzoli, who somehow knew exactly what I had in mind when I first envisioned this book.

Thank you to my agent, Elizabeth Kaplan, who is my rock-solid constant cheerleader and advocate in my world of ever-changing editors and publishers.

As always, my biggest thanks goes to my family. To my parents Joseph and Ursula Helman and Barbara and Roger Wood; to my sisters Robin Helman and Jodi Helman and their families; and to all the Minchillis for sharing too many meals to count.

Thanks especially to my stepmother Ursula, for continuing to set the most beautiful tables I have the pleasure of eating at regularly: they are an inspiration. And thank you to Courtney Sale Ross who, all those many years ago, taught me the difference between a water and wine glass, and made sure I never forgot which side of the plate the fork goes on.

Finally to Domenico, Sophie, and Emma. Although I may eat out a lot, and I may also host a lot of dinners and lunches at home, the meals I spend with you three are, of course, my favorite.

ELIZABETH MINCHILLI has written about food, style, and architecture from her home in Italy for the past 25 years. Her website, Elizabeth Minchilli in Rome (elizabethminchilli.com), won a Saveur Blog Award for Best Culinary Coverage, an Italy Magazine Best Food Blog Award, and was named The Culture Trip Local Favorite. Elizabeth is the author of eight books, including *Eating My Way Through Italy*. She is also the founder of the Eat Italy app. Her books, blogs, apps, and food tours have been praised by *The New York Times*, *Los Angeles Times*, *Travel & Leisure*, *NPR*, *The Huffington Post*, *Condé Nast Traveler*, and more.